PENGUIN BO

Healing Ways

Dr Robin Kelly was born in North London in 1951, studying medicine at the Middlesex Hospital Medical School. After three years in hospital medicine, he emigrated to Auckland, New Zealand, eventually settling into general practice in 1981. Faced with managing a large practice with many patients dependent on prescription medicines, he started to explore other, more holistic, ways to help them. Together with a small group of like-minded doctors, he studied acupuncture preferring to honour the classical Chinese approach, adapting it to treat contemporary ill health. As President of the Medical Acupuncture Society (NZ) he helped co-ordinate teaching programmes for doctors in New Zealand, liaising closely with medical and physiotherapy groups in Australia, Canada and the United States. He travelled extensively pursuing his studies including a time in Chinese hospitals.

Over recent years, he has adapted his practice using a complementary mixture of Western, Eastern and modern mindbody medicine. Together with Dr Tim Ewer from Nelson, he runs workshops internationally, teaching health professionals practical ways of introducing these concepts into the modern setting.

He is also a musician and singer/songwriter. His first album of original songs was released in 1998, receiving national radio and television exposure. He lives with his wife and three children in Takapuna, on Auckland's North Shore.

I work and write from home; the unconditional love of my wife Trish, my daughters Sophie and Lucy, my son Toby, and our dog George constantly enriches me and all who pass through our doors. You'll find its warm glow reflected on every page.

Healing Ways

A doctor's guide to healing

Dr Robin Kelly F.R.N.Z.C.G.P.

PENGUIN BOOKS

PENGUIN BOOKS

Penguin Books (NZ) Ltd, cnr Airborne and Rosedale Roads, Albany,
Auckland 1310, New Zealand
Penguin Books Ltd, 27 Wrights Lane, London W8 5TZ, England
Penguin Putnam Inc, 375 Hudson Street, New York, NY 10014, United States
Penguin Books Australia Ltd, 487 Maroondah Highway, Ringwood, Australia 3134
Penguin Books Canada Ltd, 10 Alcorn Avenue, Toronto, Ontario, Canada M4V 3B2
Penguin Books (South Africa) Pty Ltd, 5 Watkins Street,
Denver Ext 4, 2094, South Africa
Penguin Books India (P) Ltd, 11, Community Centre, Panchsheel Park,
New Delhi 110 017, India

Penguin Books Ltd, Registered Offices: Harmondsworth, Middlesex, England

First published by Penguin Books (NZ) Ltd, 2000

1 3 5 7 9 10 8 6 4 2

Copyright © Dr Robin Kelly, 2000

The right of Dr Robin Kelly to be identified as the author of this work in terms of
section 96 of the Copyright Act 1994 is hereby asserted.

Extract from *Cold Mountain* by Charles Frazier is reproduced by kind permission
of Hodder and Stoughton Limited.
Extract from *The Tibetan Book of Living and Dying* by Soygal Rinpoche is reproduced
by kind permission of Rigpa International.
Extract from Dr Larry Dossey is reproduced by kind permission of author.
Extract from *New Scientist* is reproduced by kind permission
of the magazine, www.newscientist.com

Designed by Mary Egan
Typeset by Egan-Reid Ltd, Auckland
Illustrations by Sandy Collins
Printed in Australia by Australian Print Group, Maryborough

All rights reserved. Without limiting the rights under copyright reserved above,
no part of this publication may be reproduced, stored in or introduced
into a retrieval system, or transmitted, in any form or by any means
(electronic, mechanical, photocopying, recording or otherwise), without
the prior written permission of both the copyright owner and
the above publisher of this book.

ISBN 0 14 029693 X

Contents

Acknowledgements

This book represents a tree of living knowledge. To some it will provide shelter and to some energy. Some may wish to climb it and explore; some may even look out from the uppermost branches to embrace sights previously hidden from view. I have been privileged to be its curator – along with a powerful and sensitive team of friends.
My thanks go to you all.

To Susan Reardon who helped provide a special space for our tree to grow.

To Tania Clifton-Smith, and Dr John Wellingham who were there when the seed was sown.

To my patient guides who have provided such rich stable soil for strong roots to take hold.

To the quoted writers, scientists, doctors and philosophers who have instilled our tree with their noble presence.

To the wise doctors – Tim Ewer, Marc Cohen, Gerald Gibb, Steven Aung, Richard Fox, Roger Booth and Robert Biggs – who have watered and (organically) fertilised the roots.

To my talented author friends – Anne Marie Yockney, Neil Robinson, Shelley Warner and Allan Coulam – who have nurtured and counselled the 'green' curator.

To my mentors – Genevieve Wardrop, Judy McInnarney, Jan Mitchell, Denise Barlow, Chree Barker, Angela Walters, Linda Stuckey, Julie Ewer and Judi Grace – who have been content to let the branches sway in the wind.

To artist Sandy Collins and typesetter Mary Egan who have allowed the tree to blossom through a delicate infusion of their special talents.

Special thanks to my editors at Penguin Books New Zealand – Bernice Beachman and Philippa Gerrard – for their prudent pruning; and moreover for their faith, humour and encouragement.

And to my wife Trish for her patience, her understanding and her love.

Foreword

There are many modalities of healing for human beings. Recognition of this has recently come to be termed complementary or integrative medicine. The guiding force behind these initiatives — which will undoubtedly gain momentum throughout the 21st century and indeed the 3rd millennium — is that healing is not merely a technical phenomenon, but a holistic process of facilitating peace, happiness and harmony. Physicians are not superior to their patients. Both must work together with an attitude of mutual honour and respect. Dr Robin Kelly's medical work and this present book, *Healing Ways — A Doctor's Guide to Healing*, embodies this vitally important perspective.

This book is definitely required reading for patients, physicians and health care professionals everywhere who are deeply interested in the art of healing. I really appreciate Robin's direct, people-centered approach. It is what used to be called merely clinical, but here it approaches the 'super natural' clinical. For example, from engaging Harry, a 52-year-old patient suffering from the early symptoms of heart disease due to smoking, he proceeds to a thoughtful meditation on overcoming fear in relation to cancer sufferers.

Thanks to Robin for his down-to-earth, case-study and analytic approach. I believe this has always been the heart and soul of family medicine and will remain a permanent commitment. Medicine should not have any divisions, east, west, north or south. It should always be aimed toward the total health and well-being of all our dear patients. In classical physics it is a fact that for every action there is an equal and opposite reaction. It is the same in medicine — qualitatively speaking. As physicians and practitioners of primary care, we must take care to

9

make our healing encounters the very best experience for all concerned within the context of the vital energy given to us from our mother nature. The essence of this sacred quest is to honour and respect our patients as our best friends and honoured teachers. Indeed, the most 'difficult' patients are our most valued teachers.

Steven K. H. Aung

MD, FAAFP, FICAE, Associate Clinical Professor, Departments of Medicine and Family Medicine and Adjunct Professor of Extension, University of Alberta, Edmonton, Alberta, Canada; Associate Clinical Professor, New York University College of Dentistry, New York, United States; President, Canadian Medical Acupuncture Society; President, World Natural Medicine Foundation, Edmonton, Alberta, Canada

Introduction

For over 10 years I have been asked to treat people who have failed to become well despite the best medical care available. The chronically ill, the perpetually stressed, and those in constant pain appear at my home with letters from their doctor, specialist, physiotherapist or chiropractor. They are greeted by my wife, our visually impaired cocker spaniel George and our two-year-old son who for a month has assumed the persona of the Caped Crusader from Gotham City. They will also be instantly aware of the presence of our teenage daughters if they are anywhere in the house.

The letters from these reputable, caring health professionals frequently explain the fate of the person present. That despite the latest medications, state-of-the-art computerised scans and skilful, delicate surgery all is still not well. In fact often things are worse. Some, kindly, think I may be able to help. Some, almost as kindly, can't think of anywhere else to send them.

Other folk arrive with no letter. They have been told they can't get any better. They are not so sure of this themselves. Could they talk about it?

I greet them with that standard medical apology, 'I'm running a wee bit late today.' We sit down and talk. They look around often in the hope of spying some sparkling piece of equipment that they last saw on '60 Minutes' with a leading pain specialist from Seattle at the controls. They do see some machines, but they look strangely old and unused. I explain that they are indeed old and unused. That I can offer in their place time and patience, and that half a dozen small disposable steel pins may help them begin to feel better.

Our lives have become increasingly complex. Many illnesses that linger don't seem to make any sense. They make us feel heavy, useless, muddled and old. We'd like to forget about our bodies for a while, and have a laugh, dance and whistle like we used to. They are soon sending a man (or woman) to Mars; so why is my backache such a problem?

The aim of this book is to inform and guide. There will be no rigid formulae, no cookbook recipes. I wish simply to allow the reader to gain comfort from the breadth of wisdom that now abounds on healing: from the East and the West, from the past and the present, from science and from literature.

The healing stories will show us how to overcome the barriers to healing. Scientific research will give us confidence in our journeys, while Chinese medicine will provide us with a valid working model of healing. Together we will explore the frontiers of modern scientific theory, which are leading us to even deeper levels of understanding of natural healing.

The healing value of relationships is a recurring theme. Relationships within our own bodies, with friends and loved ones, and nature itself. We can no longer be viewed as 'closed' isolated systems; our connections reach far and wide, through and beyond the limits of our senses.

The exercises are simple and fun. Adapt them so you own them — let them become part of your day-to-day life. In my experience, many techniques are unduly complex, and we become sidetracked by the details. These rituals should act as antidotes to the competitiveness and pressures of our lives. Please relax and enjoy them. Even allow yourself a chuckle while you do them.

I see no conflict between the aims of this book and the goals of quality modern healthcare. No good doctor prescribes unnecessary medicines or advises surgery without weighing up all other options. This is not a shot fired in anger despite certain frustrations I have with current health policies worldwide. My wife, who had a serious haemorrhage after the birth of our son, and my daughter who had severe bronchopneumonia at the age of 11 months owe their lives to modern medical techniques, and the necessary reductionist principles involved in their development and practice.

However, it still seems to be all too common that we embark on complex surgery or drug regimens without paying due attention to the potential blocks the patient has to deep healing. Unresolved grief, unhappy relationships, or ailing loved ones are all situations known to delay healing. Many people presenting to me with post-operative pain and complications have not been given the opportunity to explore these links. Repeat operations are too often performed instead, further delaying and complicating healing. Such stories appear throughout this book.

My wish, though, is to be the bearer of good news. A healthy optimist, a harbinger of true, not false hope. Like all family doctors, I have been immensely fortunate. I have been allowed to share the most intimate and joyful times with all manner of people, as if I were a trusted friend or family member.

I have been confided in, and had the privilege of imparting news, good and bad, that will affect lives significantly. I have been present when lives enter this world, and when they depart. I have frequently observed how light and precious life seems; and how dark and burdensome illness is in contrast. Puzzling, complicated and illogical.

Healing frees us from these chains. A simple process leading to a simple but profound conclusion — a return to the pure state of health.

I hope this book gives confidence to all who wish to re-own their healing. This, surely, is the right of us all.

The language of healing

Through this book, I intend to impart my understanding of the healing process based on my experiences and studies. There exists in my mind no conflict between curing and healing. We are not dealing with *alternative medicine*, but an approach to health that complements and enriches good, modern healthcare.

Healing is re-emerging as a medical term meaning more than the healthy resolution of a physical wound. Family doctors are becoming more comfortable in using the term *holistically*, although I am still politely warned by friendly specialists not to mention the 'H-word' within the hallowed walls of our local teaching hospital! I am increasingly intrigued to observe how different health professions cope with this term. Research papers in the medical literature still reflect the formal approach of the resolution of a physical wound. Try typing *healing* into any reputable medical internet website and you will discover this for yourselves. Mainstream psychology has a similar blindspot to deeper aspects of healing, although I have found many practising psychologists both intrigued and frustrated by this.

In marked contrast, nursing journals are literally overflowing with expanded views of healing — healing journeys, listening, touching, etc. Similarly, the ever-increasing numbers of quality, complementary journals embrace these concepts of healing. The references quoted in this book come from all these reputable sources.

So how should we best define healing? Ironically, as a doctor I may be the least equipped to deliver on this — people in a *healed* state have tended to keep away from us. I am always overjoyed to receive a call from well patients, often months, even years after I had last seen them. I am vividly reminded of Jane, who fractured her spine in a helicopter accident in which her fiancé was tragically killed. Her spine was supported by metal rods internally, and Jane was in constant severe pain. I did as best I could several years ago to ease her pain, as one of her 'team'.

Jane wrote to me last year from Washington DC. Inside the envelope was a photograph of a beaming Jane, surrounded by her new husband and two children.

Healing is not just a medical term. It means returning to a state of joy, harmony and health; a state of being where life has meaning and purpose.

In recent years, there has been continuing debate on the correct usage of the labels previously ascribed to both the givers and receivers of healthcare. As we learn more about holistic healing methods, we see these boundaries become increasingly blurred. The patriarchal image of a doctor is being challenged, with an overwhelming, truly healthy move to regard the relationship as a partnership. The growth in complementary practitioners worldwide has both reflected this and guided the nursing and medical professions towards adopting this holistic model.

The healer and the healed walk parallel paths. As healing progresses, through formal and informal contacts with family, friends and fellow sufferers, there is a cascade of influence which is deeply satisfying to all concerned. However, for reasons of simplicity — and the fact that I am yet to find better terms — I will often use the terms *patient* and *healer*.

Several years ago, there was a definite attempt to rename the receivers of healthcare *clients*. This appeared to be a reaction against the paternalistic, doctor-dominated role. I remember being unhappy about this term, as not only did the word *client* suggest a primarily commercial partnership, it left behind a sense of softness and comfort which I had experienced myself in the role of a *patient*. This word is derived from the Latin verb *patere*, to suffer, and I feel that acknowledging the suffering of those seeking help is far from patronising. The issue seems to be how we, as doctors, responded to such suffering.

In my view all health workers and healers — be they body workers, osteopaths, nurses, physiotherapists, chiropractors or doctors — aim to lessen human suffering by interacting with *patients*.

The term *healer* implies no innate superiority. There are no 'superstar' healers. All living beings are in a constant state of healing, healing themselves and all who come into contact with them. It is a natural living state, common to men, women and children, dogs and cats, plants and trees. Our complicated lives have often made us lose touch with our potential to heal; but the skills are easily relearned if we are open to them.

The concepts, stories and exercises in this book will be relevant to all in 'less than perfect' health. However, the extent of the effects will vary from condition to condition. We now have cures for diseases that were previously fatal; antibiotics prevent death from meningitis, pneumonia and septicaemia; many cancers are now curable through early detection, sophisticated drugs and surgery. Expert control of diabetes mellitus with medicine and insulin now allows diabetics a quality of life denied to them in less enlightened times. For these and many other people, modern *biomedicine* provides the lifeline.

This book addresses how we can create the best environment to heal. The existing model of disease often sees the body in a state of war, under attack from a foreign invader, maybe a virus or bacterium. If a country is invaded, it not only arms its military with powerful weapons to ward off these unwanted intruders, its politicians also make sure that the population is adequately fed, free of disease and supports its army.

Not only is the invasion quashed, but strength and prosperity is retained in the land. So it is with our bodies; even those with illnesses strongly reliant on medical cures will benefit from knowledge gained in this book. But there are many others who remain unwell despite the best efforts of 'mainstream' treatments. Some cannot tolerate their medication; some are even made worse by their treatment or develop new conditions as a result.

Many more feel awful, tired, or pained without a reasonable diagnosis, let alone a cure. They have had many opinions from different doctors, friends, complementary practitioners and others. For this large group, understanding and regaining control of their own healing is essential. Over the years I have seen many whose health has returned and been less dependent on powerful drugs, as these insights have evolved. Some of their stories are in this book.

Strong evidence is now emerging that our minds do not reside solely in our brains: that every other cell in our body is involved in the workings of our mind, in our survival and our healing. We think consciously with our brain, and the body's messages are unscrambled and organised by our brain, but there is also a network of communication involved between all our cells that is an integral part of our mind, the *bodymind*. We feel with our bodies.

The linking of emotions to healing continues to cause concern to many inside and outside orthodox medicine. The most frequent adverse comment is that, by linking causes of illness to emotions, one can lay the patient open to feelings of guilt and inadequacy about getting the disease in the first place. That somehow their suffering is a punishment for past mistakes. This is, of course, unhelpful and ultimately unhealthy. As the stories in this book show, this direct 'cause and effect' is too simplistic: most people I see are sensitive, caring and loving. Usually, they have spent their lives giving out more compassion and energy than they have received. Many have been the victims of circumstances beyond their control. Some have inherited traits. Some have simply been unlucky.

Healing does not involve judging a person, only helping and guiding. The mindbody approach should be owned, understood and used by one's own self.

1. *My story*

Men in their generations are like the leaves of the trees. The wind blows and one year's leaves are scattered on the ground; but the trees burst into bud and put on fresh ones when the spring comes round.

— HOMER, c. 900 BC

I grew up in a medical household. My father was a family doctor in suburban London, and the surgery was next to our dining room. It was a comfortable, warm, busy home. Gentleness, kindness and soft humour eased effortlessly from my Irish father. His father had been a Protestant minister in the predominantly working-class Catholic town of Dungiven in Northern Ireland. He had conducted the memorial services in Belfast for the crew members lost at sea when the *Titanic* sank in 1912.

As well as running a busy household, my mother single-handedly ran the practice for many years in a job that would now be collectively held by nurses, receptionists, commercial cleaners and practice managers. She tells me she is still recovering.

Her mother was the very first Montessori teacher in England. She studied under Professor Montessori in Italy in her early twenties, before World War I, setting up the first school in wooden huts in the grounds of King Alfred's School in Golders Green, North London. During the war she joined the St John Ambulance Brigade. She nursed with them until she was 85. My grandmother's family were Quakers.

I felt comfortable at the thought of being a doctor, and I can't remember any pressure from my family. My brother and sister took different paths. At boarding school, I loved the classics: Homer's *Iliad*, Ovid, Latin verse, scanning and translation. I only remember seeking career advice once, from my Latin and English teacher. I had written an essay on the similarities I had perceived between the structure of atoms and solar systems. This precocious 'stab in the dark' at a great unifying theory I thought had literary merit; he quietly advised me to be a doctor. I was fourteen.

The subject I disliked most was physics, a necessary hurdle to gaining entrance to medical school. I found it dry and uninteresting and it was with great relief that I scraped through the A level, with the sincere hope I would never open a physics book again.

My house is now littered with physics books, and I would strongly suggest to anyone with a similar school experience to start again with Einstein's theory of relativity, and to work backwards (and forwards) from there. It is a shame that school physics stops just when it becomes interesting. I suspect that there is still a feeling that concepts such as probability, chaos and relativity lack the hard discipline of Newtonian physics and are somehow unsuitable for secondary school minds. Maybe it's because these concepts are about releasing control and freeing our thoughts, and that this threatens those who see the world and cosmos defined by static rules. It goes a long way in explaining why it has taken nearly a century to incorporate this new world view into medicine, and why biophysics is still not included in medical school curricula.

Smells are emotive. Without being able to describe them adequately with words, one whiff can instantly take us back years in time. The memory of smells is stored mostly in the limbic system of the brain, the centre co-ordinating our survival instincts. The olfactory nerve is one of the shortest in the body with a direct route to this database. Pregnant women become highly sensitive to smells early in pregnancy as their bodies are alerted to toxins which could harm their developing child. Our pet cocker spaniel, George, is losing his sight and hearing, but will manage unless he loses his sense of smell. Smells reinforce the memory of events and emotions, and are used to great effect by aromatherapists. Acupuncturists burn the herb *artemesis* (moxa punk) on their needles, not just for the soothing heat, but to reinforce the body's memory of healing.

The smell of formalin instantly reconnects me to the moment I entered the anatomy dissection room my first day as a medical student one month after my eighteenth birthday. I was confronted by row upon row of grey, stiff human cadavers with the air dank from the overpowering rancid fumes. We were requested not to discuss this part of our studies with non-medical students. This had the effect of burying thoughts and discourse 'underground', at the same time promoting the famous 'black humour' of medical students. It also imprinted on our impressionable minds the image of dead, stringy tissue and bodies devoid of life and soul. I am sure that I took away from my dissection year many valuable lessons, not least the unconditional kindness of the donors, but I am left with a great concern that even now medical students are exposed to disturbing sights and situations without free access to spiritual counselling.

Early in my first year I heard that my best friend at school had been killed in a head-on collision. My work in hospices in recent years has highlighted our deficiencies in dealing with death. I am sure such experiences in doctors' formative years have contributed to this in no small way.

Fear of death is seen as a necessary part of modern medicine; we talk of five-year survival figures in cancer; our cures save lives; smallpox has been eradicated by effective vaccination. A cancer patient I saw recently had just been told of her diagnosis the previous week. The doctor had appeared at the consulting room door, after reviewing her test results in another room.

'*I'm afraid it's bad news. It's definitely cancer*,' he said, avoiding eye contact.

The lady, who remains both positive and philosophical, felt uneasy for him and despite respecting his expertise was unwilling to see him again. Being a very giving person, she felt the need to support him and reassure him in his fear. The words 'I'm afraid . . .' couldn't be undone.

My clinical training was thorough, but focused on patients with advanced stages of diseases requiring radical therapies in hospital. Working in a famous London teaching hospital meant that many of the conditions were rare; many I haven't encountered since.

Our first day's lectures included the sombre warning: 'Don't allow yourself to become emotionally involved.'

Already I felt the messages were different from those that I had somehow absorbed in my childhood. The early 1970s were years of great promise for the pharmaceutical industry with blood-pressure drugs, tranquillisers, anti-depressants and many new antibiotics coming onto

the market. I remember being overwhelmed by much of this information, and even more so by their potential side effects.

I was also introduced to the word *placebo*, the term used to describe
the beneficial, psychological effects of prescribing a drug which could
not be explained by its chemistry. Trials designed to exclude this curious
effect, using identical but chemically inactive control pills, were being
conducted by respected clinicians. Yet I found it difficult to understand
why the effect of placebo — the Latin for *I shall please* — was regarded
with such suspicion. Surely anything as mysterious as this that could
account for a positive response in 30–60 percent[1, 2] of patients should
be investigated, understood and enhanced. (Progress is still slow on this
for many reasons, but we will examine the placebo effect in greater depth
in Chapter 4.)

After qualifying, I was unsure whether to specialise or go into general
practice. I knew my father's practice would be available if I so wished,
although I had been somewhat discouraged by the short, pressured
consultation times that seemed the rule in the National Health Service.
After my pre-registration (intern) year, I pursued my interest in
paediatrics (sick children) and oncology (cancer treatment with radiotherapy and chemotherapy). Busy, intense and demanding work that I
found satisfying despite the long hours. I was recently married and living
almost out of a suitcase as the jobs rarely lasted for more than six
months. In 1977 I answered an advertisement in the *British Medical
Journal* for a job in Auckland, New Zealand combining paediatrics and
oncology, and duly arrived in what was to become our new home later
that year.

I enjoyed my five years in hospital medicine, but was concerned that
the way to progress was to sub-specialise and that there were real risks
of becoming distanced from the underlying causes of illness. Of course,
with the huge advance in knowledge and the sophistication of surgical
techniques this has all been necessary. It was just that it didn't feel right
for me.

I was impressed that general practice was less restricted in New
Zealand, with many doctors running 15-minute consultations rather
than the five minutes often encountered in England at that time. In June
1981, after a year of specific training in family medicine, I was content

to settle into the life of a general practitioner in the comfortable seaside suburb of Takapuna on Auckland's North Shore.

One of my new partners, Doug Carnachan, had a special interest in acupuncture. He had spent some time in China and had successfully integrated it into his practice. He was treating mainly painful conditions — injuries, arthritis, headaches, etc. — with success. What impressed me was not only his integrity but the patients' obvious enthusiasm for this strange 'new' treatment.

Unknown to me at the time, Doug was unwell. Nine months later, at the age of 40, he died suddenly while touring England.

The doctors who have influenced me the most are a rare breed. Not only have they had an expert's grasp of their specialty, they have also been great listeners. This is, I'm sure, a sign of humility; all are or were humble.

> 'In name there are many doctors but in reality only a few.'
>
> — Hippocratic Corpus, 400 BC

Doug and my good friend Gerald Gibb, the pioneering 'father of New Zealand acupuncture', would certainly have qualified for entry into Hippocrates' inner circle at the School of Cos. Gerald has introduced over 400 doctors to acupuncture through his teaching courses over the past quarter of a century. Both Doug and Gerald were my trusted guides and mentors, encouraging me in those early years by the examples they set.

I also had many patients who were keen to see me start. I felt immediately comfortable with acupuncture — not only because of Doug and Gerald but also because of its obvious staying power in the world's largest nation.

I was drawn to the holistic Taoist philosophies, the Laws of the Five Elements, the macrocosm expressed in the microcosm of the body, the focus on natural healing.

What's more it seemed to work.

I attended courses and started to use it on simple acute conditions which, in my early zeal, frequently responded instantly. In retrospect, I chose these conditions wisely — stiff necks, stuck backs, etc. Quite apart from the instant feedback, more than a few patients reported other pleasant changes they attributed to the treatments. Hot flushes seemed to lose their fire, irritable bowels were calmed, and sleep patterns improved. This was pleasing to all concerned, and I gratefully basked in the mild degree of adulation I received as a result. However, inwardly I was rather bemused. These were often conditions I had no idea I was treating.

Even more intriguing were my observations that these pioneering patients often began to lead fuller lives. They procrastinated less; undone things were done; they felt more like 'their old selves'. Acupuncture was giving me a new, expanded view on *wellness*.

Nevertheless, the reasons for improvement, which were far from universal, remained mysterious. And this was despite my delving into as many acupuncture and Chinese medical books as I could lay my hands on. By the late eighties, it seemed to click. Workshops on the *zang-fu* — the body/mind/spirit relationship of the Chinese syndromes — rang true. These associations were ones I had encountered time and again in hospital and family practice. As an invited professor recounted these links, it seemed to make instant sense as memories of past patients' illnesses gained new, expanded meanings. She described in detail the ways different emotions and climatic conditions could, according to the Chinese, influence the body; that different organ systems were affected by different conditions, and that many of the diseases we treat in the West are seen as the *biao* (branch) of deeper problems in the *ben* (root). With this new knowledge, I began to treat more complex problems for which Western medicine could offer at the most only symptomatic relief.

And a new word had re-entered my vocabulary — *healing*.

Adapting this holistic model of health to the structure of general practice was becoming increasingly difficult. I had a busy full-time practice, a post as medical officer to multi-handicapped children and also a growing interest in the care of the dying. My enthusiasm for Chinese and holistic medicine was driving me to reassess my roles. It required my total focus at consultation times; distractions such as phone interruptions, the increasing paper war and time constraints all worked against my attempt to create a gentle healing environment.

So I sold up, and in 1991 created a new non-prescribing holistic practice in purpose-built rooms attached to our home.

By this time I was receiving more referrals from doctors and other health professionals, with many patients having failed to respond to 'conventional' approaches. I wrote to all my general practice patients individually, asking them to understand my new role, and thanking them for the lessons they had taught me. This was the most difficult part, and I was surprised by the grief I felt at 'losing them'. Although deep grief usually results from losing a dear friend or family member, severing the subtle healing links between myself and 2000 friends was far from easy. I yearned for the most mundane, quick consultations; for a short while I even craved the instant satisfaction of successfully syringing out ear wax! The first patient who came to my new practice I assessed as being unsuitable for treatment. After recommending another approach and seeing him on his way with gentle reassurance, I retired to the bedroom, clutched my head and wept loudly. By lunchtime I felt considerably better.

If the eighties was the decade that opened many of us up to different paradigms of health, the nineties was to show us how best to adapt these to modern patterns of illness. The existing reductionist, allopathic approach was being challenged not just by an increasingly aware public but by respected scientists, doctors and the growing number of natural health practitioners. Links were being made between ancient Eastern philosophies and modern physics; an endocrinologist (hormone specialist) Deepak Chopra explained meditation in the language of quantum physics in his book *Quantum Healing*, and physicist Fritjof Capra explored the similarities between Taoist philosophy and new physics in *The Tao of Physics*. The holistic world view of James Lovelock, whose *Gaia Theory* saw earth as one living organism, was being taken seriously by a growing number of informed educated people.

My new practice grew rapidly, and those coming to me fell roughly into two categories. First, there were those who reflected the growing awareness in holistic principles, the health conscious. By and large they appreciated the reassurance of having a therapist and guide in complementary medicine who had also had an 'orthodox' training. This group continue to provide me with stimulation and satisfaction, with their sense of personal responsibility and enquiring nature. I have found that the vast majority of those who use complementary approaches alongside 'conventional medicine' do so with great commonsense and safety. I have made it a priority to foster good relationships with both the medical and natural health communities, and have often acted as a 'go-between' for these groups.

Secondly, there were those chronically ill who had 'failed' to respond to both orthodox and other treatments. Patients with chronic pain, chronic fatigue, severe overuse syndromes, arthritis and many conditions that had defied diagnosis. The challenge was how to best use my acupuncture skills, and my own growing consciousness for the benefit of those unfortunate people.

The most common ingredient missing from their care, I discovered, was themselves.

Often the good intentions of medical professionals attempting to *manage* a condition lead to a *lack of participation* by the sufferer. By interfering with this personal responsibility, the patient's confidence and ability to heal are often eroded. These patients feel failures, incurable and despondent. It was clear that acupuncture could do only so much for this group. Although it, together with a Chinese medical history and diagnosis, has much to offer in achieving a balance — a state of peace in the body and mind — my real goal was to induce a state of deep self-healing.

My own experiences were mirroring exciting developments in an emerging medical discipline — *psycho-neuro-immunology* (PNI) — which was discovering links between our emotions, our nervous system and our immune system. For the rest of the book I will substitute this rather cumbersome, jargonised term with the simpler, more holistic term *mindbody medicine*. Mindbody medicine embraces the theory that our body has a mind of its own — outside the direct control of our brain — a 'subconscious' system of communication, the *bodymind*, distinct from the 'conscious' mind of the brain.

'Hard' evidence was emerging from highly respected research groups on the effect of emotions on healing. Dr David Spiegel of Harvard produced a landmark study, published in *The Lancet*, showing the effects of a well-facilitated support group on patients with breast cancer.[3]

This had been formed primarily to support them through the rigours of surgery, radiation and chemotherapy. The unexpected finding, when the study was evaluated several years later, was that the 'survival' times of these cancer sufferers had doubled. Something significant had happened to their healing from the interactions associated with this group. This has been just one of many studies that have spurred a new interest in the healing effects of interactions between individuals, not just those involving health professionals. The powerful effects of *listening* are being taken seriously again, not just from anecdotal evidence but from quality research.[4]

My move to create more time, essential to listening, made real sense. I began to look at consultations in a new light. With this new evidence and my interest in ancient, time-honoured healing practice, I was seeing the consultation more in terms of a healing *ritual*. (We will explore how this knowledge can enhance the value of the time the healer and patient spend together in Chapters 4 and 10.)

❧

As the word *healing* begins to find its place again in doctors' vocabulary, even more tentatively comes the word *spirituality*. Unfortunately, all those within the medical profession who have expressed an interest in holistic matters have been greeted with varying degrees of resistance. Most will tell you of incidents of public derision, even when the scientific research is impressive. No more has this been so than for those exploring spirituality.

I was fortunate to be asked to act as medical director of our local hospice for care of the dying in 1992, as it expanded from a home-care service to a fully fledged inpatient and outpatient unit. On reflection I have been drawn in my career into the care of patients at times in their lives when their own egos are less likely to impose themselves on a healing relationship.

Children, the handicapped and the dying share the gift of honesty, which makes the job of trying to help them such a privilege. Working with the dying has given me more insights into spiritual matters than any other area.

In dying, healing is at its most profound.

The brave pioneers of palliative care have not only reduced the suffering of dying; they have opened our eyes to the spiritual dimensions of living. The teachings of Elisabeth Kübler-Ross and Eric Cassell are two of many in this field that I have found enlightening. I have learned much from the dying, and their healing stories act as a source of inspiration for all of us.

❧

My continuing goal has been to adapt the healing techniques I am experienced in to facilitate a deep level of healing. Patients should re-own their healing with daily routines which honour and promote this. We should feel a sense of sharing with the procedures used, which should be easily understood and above all painless. We should be free to laugh, have fun and discuss spiritual issues.

The evolution from curing to healing requires me to keep a constant vigil on myself. The close connections made in all healing encounters are profound, and practising the exercises described in this book has been essential for maintaining my own health. Focus on the breath always brings me in touch with the present, and simple meditation helps me stand outside my own, and others' worries and fears.

The practice of *qi-gong* combines exercise, meditation and visualisation and I am indebted to my friend and qi-gong master Dr Steven Aung from Edmonton, Canada, who has done much to introduce this to Western health professionals. His teachings on how we can draw from our natural environment to assist us to gain energy and balance have been a revelation for me. The accumulated effect of this awareness has been an essential part of my growth. It has also helped me tune into the extreme subtlety of living energy systems, and honour the widely differing levels of sensitivity we all possess.

I have had to adopt these exercises for my own health. My work brings me so close to pain and fatigue that I suffer these symptoms myself, if I am not vigilant. Over the years, this has been a very real problem for me. Like most modern Westerners, I had not learned to look after myself. The pace of my life, my unreasonable personal expectations and my competitive nature have all needed to be balanced. Finding the time and motivation to allow even 10 minutes of silence per day is not easy as these traits seem so deeply instilled. And like so many patients seeing me, I have consulted doctors and complementary practitioners, had tests, read books and searched my soul. And yes, I have frequently given myself acupuncture. For years I was reluctant to tell patients of my struggles. I now know the importance of sharing these experiences; in some cases it is vital if we are to form a bond that is potentially healing. Most need to know I take my own advice. And how I, too, struggle to get it right.

This is now the *information* age. I have been intrigued and dazzled by the explosion of information technology and the theories used in developing these advances. Information theory is now at the cutting edge of scientific research, and I am excited by the many insights this is giving us into healing. Symptoms are messages, our bodies' means of communication — a true non-verbal expression of our *bodymind*. They can be seen in the light of the information they convey to us, and information theory is helping us unravel some of the mysteries of the healing process.

By applying this theory to my own work, I find it simplifies and demystifies some aspects of healing. For example, with acupuncture, I am able to use tiny needles which seem to act as *conductors* of information between the patient's body and the outside environment often via myself. Frequently, simple touch is enough. The key is to tune in to the body's messages — first 'listen' before 'replying'.

It is like dealing with a small child. If we try to control the *bodymind*, it doesn't play ball! When approached with compassion and trust, our healing intent can be transformed into reality through simple means. This is one beginning to self-healing.

I feel fortunate to have been able to watch the progress of 'chronically ill' patients as a doctor, without the pressure to prescribe. In this setting, I have been free to explore the meaning of symptoms, seeing them in the overall context of healing — an interpreter rather than interrogator. I have been able to observe the subtlety of healing, as patients leave behind the controlling chaos of chronic illness and embark on their journeys of self-discovery. It continues to be a privilege to accompany them along the way.

2. Clearing the way

$\mathcal{O}$ur bodies continually talk to us. If I am hungry, hunger messages are sent to me by my stomach. If I ignore them — I may be listening intently to a patient or be totally immersed in a football game — my guts start making a noise. Not only do they let me know their wishes, but anyone near me is also aware and frequently highly amused.

There are many reasons that prevent us listening to the needs of our bodies. The stressful conditions of today's work environment is an obvious example. If our bodies continue to be ignored, the messages can become more complex and difficult to fix. Stomachs that have not been listened to may produce more acid which is not neutralised by food. Gastritis, or even an ulcer may result. We now know that each cell lining our gut is laced with receptors which respond to molecules produced by different emotional states. These chemicals were previously called *neuropeptides* because we used to think such chemicals were only produced by the brain and nervous system. Now conclusive evidence is emerging that cells throughout the body both produce and receive messages from these chemicals, now renamed simply *peptides*.[5]

Orthodox medicine is now referring to this phenomenon as the *gut brain*. It is particularly active if we are caught up in a situation over which we have little control such as when we have to suppress our emotions or how we feel. Our bodies don't like the fact that we are having no say in our own welfare. If our voices are not being heard, our *bodymind* lets us know. Its sole interest is our survival.

So how can we begin to address this confusion in our lives?

Let's start by examining the events and situations that are preventing our bodies from being heard. There is now strong medical evidence that simply taking this step of recognition can have a remarkable effect on the body. It has been shown that writing down an account of the stresses in our lives can improve our immunity to disease, and lessen the symptoms of illnesses such as asthma and rheumatoid arthritis. A 1995 study performed by Drs Roger Booth and Keith Petrie at Auckland Medical School involved medical students writing down accounts of the most stressful times in their past, prior to receiving immunisations to protect them from the occupational hazard of Hepatitis B.[6] The effectiveness of the immunisation in each student was checked four and six months later by measuring the specific antibody levels in blood samples. Those students who had been involved in the exercise showed significantly better immune responses than a control group who were asked to write on other topics.

In an even more recent study, patients with asthma or rheumatoid arthritis underwent a similar exercise.[7] Those who wrote about the most stressful event in their lives were compared with those who wrote about 'emotionally neutral topics'. Four months later the two groups were studied in relation to their particular symptoms. The researchers measured the peak flow — the amount of air breathed out in a single breath — in the patients with asthma, and subjected those who had rheumatoid arthritis to a symptom questionnaire. They found that the lung measurements had improved by 15 percent in the 'asthmatics' who wrote of their stresses. It stayed the same in the other group. Those with rheumatoid arthritis also benefited from the exercise. Forty-seven percent showed improved symptoms compared with 24 percent of the control group.

It is not known whether these effects will last, but it is certainly encouraging news.

This experiment also shows another common finding: that a number of people participating in such a trial improve even in a control group subjected to an intervention we suspect has little obvious benefit. Twenty-four percent of the arthritis sufferers improved for no obvious reason. This is termed the *placebo* effect. It is important for us to understand the reasons for this, as we should endeavour to enhance it as much as we can. It is safe and cheap. Unfortunately, many doctors have been trained to see it only as something to measure the effectiveness of a treatment against. We have to prove the effect of a drug against this placebo and so it has tended to be treated as a necessary, but rather unwelcome guest by researchers trying to prove the worth of a new drug. The term *'just a placebo'* is frequently used as a term of derision for unproven interventions, especially if they involve subtle interaction between patient and therapist. For those participating in clinical trials, we can see many potential reasons why beneficial placebo effects occur.

People love helping others. They become the *wounded healers*, and evidence shows that this is truly healing for themselves. All religions recognise this; Buddhists describe this as the state of *tonglen*.[8] We have all experienced how uplifting it can be to help someone out of a tricky situation, or even just give a word of praise and encouragement to someone down on their luck.

Clinical trials also give participants a sense of belonging, and comradeship. They are part of a group of fellow sufferers, under the guidance of a compassionate and skilled physician. They can tell their story, and be listened to. And what's more, it's free!

Being supported and belonging to a group is now seen as important for healing. Those who have a wide variety of social ties, such as close family, workmates, social and sporting clubs, have been shown to be more resistant to the common cold.[9] Breast cancer sufferers who have joined support groups have been shown not only to live better but also longer.[3]

Being ill is a very lonely place. Even your closest loved one isn't inside your skin. I have dreamed of designing and patenting a machine for the unwell. It would consist of two adhesive pads connected to a mysterious black box. One pad would be attached to you, the sufferer, and the other to someone else — someone who doesn't understand what you are going through. Possibly even your doctor. With a flick of the switch, all your symptoms could be transferred to this person. When true recognition of your suffering has been appreciated, you can show compassion and switch off. It would save much time and energy, and be an essential item in resolving compensation claims. It would, however, be rather arduous on your doctor, who may begin to adopt a more liberal policy of taking your word for your symptoms!

We live in what has been termed *The Age of Reason*.[10] Everything apparently has a cause if we can find it. Every cause has an effect. We have come to believe that for every illness, there is a cure out there waiting to be discovered. People are always asking me what is the cause of their ill health. Is it what they are eating? What are they allergic to? What have they done wrong?

Whenever anyone has presented to me with an acute allergic skin reaction, I have only rarely been able to find the exact cause. In cases of more long-standing poor health, a search for one cause is even more fruitless. Chronic illness is as complicated as life itself.

For example, *unresolved grief* plays a prominent role in many people's stories. Losing a loved one, a partner in life, is devastating enough. So often, though, it also means social isolation, being unable to overcome feelings of fear, guilt and worry. It can mean struggling to cope with wills, banks and lawyers. We may try to find comfort in alcohol, nicotine or tranquillisers. It often means burying it deep inside, as we try to get on with our busy lives.

Because of the pace of life, and the illusion of instant cause and effect, friends often mistakenly feel that in a matter of a few weeks someone will 'get over' it. But grief is as deep as love. It is a natural state that represents and honours the love shared with the person who has died. It is dynamic, changing from hour to hour, moment to moment. It is not grief itself that interferes with healing so much as our tendency to hide it. Death has been called our final *taboo*. We, as doctors, have not studied it like we have studied life. As rescuers of life, we have been conditioned to prevent death. To let a patient die is to fail.

We are confronted in the media with images of violent death. Movies have glamorised and sensationalised death, making us grateful we are sitting safely in the cinema. Death, then, becomes a violent failure that we would prefer never to experience ourselves. No wonder our friends are reluctant to bring the subject up. No wonder we fight back the tears.

Which brings me to Ruby's story:

Grief

Ruby's story

I first met Ruby in 1982, a year after I started out in general practice. Ruby was single, Scottish and in her early thirties. She appeared on the surface to be well — a bubbly, vivacious woman with a quick, dry wit. We hit it off immediately. She enjoyed jogging and was building up her road miles, dreaming of running the Boston Marathon. This she achieved in 1988. She was a successful travel agent, popular with clients and staff alike.

But hidden behind tinted glasses, her eyes told a different story. Their lids were scarred and painful. Several years earlier she had presented to a plastic surgeon with pain and a 'boggy' swelling in her eyes. The surgeon removed eyelid tissue but the symptoms worsened, and she saw another surgeon a year later. He operated again, this time using skin grafts. By the time I saw Ruby, her eyes felt tight and dry; and the pain was getting worse.

Ruby was the eighth of nine children growing up in a working-class suburb of Glasgow. Her father had left home when she was three, and her mother worked, raising the family by herself. It was a childhood with few happy memories. She fell in love with Sandy at 18, and felt truly understood for the first, and only time of her life.

She remembered having headaches at this time, over her eyes. They were bad enough for her to see her doctor for a check-up and some pills. No serious cause was found. Sandy also reassured her about them; most people, even Sandy himself, had headaches. They were blissfully happy, became engaged and married shortly before Ruby's twentieth birthday. Two weeks after the wedding, Sandy mentioned that his own headaches were worsening. One week later Sandy died suddenly.

An autopsy revealed a brain tumour.

Ruby was devastated. Lonely and with nothing to lose she emigrated to a land as far away from Glasgow as she could go — New Zealand. She worked, studied, and made new friends in a new land. However, the pains she had experienced continued spreading to her cheeks and nose. Her eyes became swollen and puffy. By the mid-1970s she had had enough, and after seeing several doctors embarked on surgery.

Ruby knew I had begun to use acupuncture, and was keen for me to try to help. It certainly did help, and during the short course of treatments I listened to the story of Ruby's difficult life.

We then lost touch, meeting up again 10 years later when her family doctor referred her back to me for more acupuncture. (I had in the meantime left my practice to 'specialise'.) The pain was bad, and she was back seeing different surgeons. She seemed deeply unhappy. Now blessed with more time in my practice at home, together we went over Ruby's life story once again. My examination revealed the same scarred eyes, and Sandy's name still on the medallion around her neck.

I explained much of what I had learned in the years since I had last seen her. The value of linking life events and traumas to one's continuing health problems, and the need to appreciate the deep effects of unresolved grief on the body. We agreed to give the healing time, always believing in the body's potential to heal. What we were to do would honour, not pressurise the body. I would give her acupuncture, and we would talk and listen. We would look for encouraging signs of healing.

After three sessions, Ruby returned overjoyed. She had had five consecutive seconds free of pain! This had not happened for 25 years.

We appeared to be on the right track.

As I treated her, we talked and joked. Despite her popularity, she had felt taken for granted in deeper relationships. None, including her present partner, remotely matched Sandy in thoughtfulness, love or consideration. As well as this, her firm had been taken over, and the new owners seemed not to appreciate her worth.

That was two years ago. Since then Ruby has changed jobs, and freed herself from her relationship. Her pain only now returns when she is under pressure. She is patiently awaiting for an advanced cosmetic surgical technique to be perfected by a surgeon she trusts.

And she has started bubbling again.

Lessons learned from Ruby

1. It's never too late to heal. Once the barriers to healing have been identified, there is no reason why we can't be optimistic about the future. Circumstances change. Both Ruby and myself became older and wiser. Age, so often seen as a barrier, can be a healer.

2. Sandy was the first, and so far the only, person who has loved, valued and appreciated Ruby. She was learning through him to love, value and appreciate herself, and then he died. She escaped across the world, but all the excitement and benefits of her new life could only bury, not resolve, her grief.

3. Her body started to talk to her. It talked to her through her eyes. I have learned through the time-honoured observations of Eastern physicians that where symptoms arise can give us great clues to the underlying causes of imbalances in the body. Both Ayurvedic and Chinese medicine have detailed the significance of symptoms occurring in various parts of the body.

   Tension builds up in the body, rising like the steam in a kettle. It tries its best to escape, often finding relief in the eyes. We often feel better after a good cry. Sometimes a good moan or shout can rid the tension. What is better than a good belly-laugh to relieve us of our worries? Ruby bottled up and coped without being able to cry safely.

4. When our body is being listened to, it gives us small but un-mistakable signs that we are on the right track. It can be that good

night's sleep we haven't had in years. Or catching ourselves singing in the shower. Or in Ruby's case, a few seconds of relief from pain. We then have to be very patient.

5. That healing, as it progresses, begins to make sense. Ruby's symptoms returned when she felt undervalued in her relationship, and when at work. The symptoms, or *bodymind*, rediscovered its role as Ruby's guide and protector.

Ruby not only had to deal with her grief but with living in a new land. Forging a new career while missing, in particular, Sandy's mother and friends. Her body did not let her forget or bury the lessons of the past.

❧

The effects of stress on wound healing

In 1995 Professor Janice Kiecolt-Glaser of the Ohio State University College of Medicine teamed up with medical and dental colleagues to study the effects on the body of looking after close relatives with Alzheimer's disease.[11] The group of 13 investigated were all women aged between 47 and 81 with an average age of 60. Nine were caring for husbands, and four for their mothers. The group was compared with a 'matched' control group, without relatives with dementia.

A surgical instrument was used to take skin samples for laboratory examination. This punched a small 3.5 mm hole in each subject's forearm, and the time taken for the wound to heal was measured in each case. Certain chemicals known as cytokines, which are known to protect against infection and prepare the injured tissue for repair were also measured.

The results were very significant. The wounds inflicted on the arms of the caregivers took nearly 10 days longer to heal than those on the controls (49 v. 39 days). The levels of cytokines were significantly less in the caregivers' group.

These results show that certain types of 'stress' may not only affect our immunity, as shown by many other trials, but also wound healing. The researchers state that 'stress-related defects in wound repair could have important clinical implications, for instance in recovery from surgery'.

❧

Looking after a loved one with Alzheimer's disease can be an immense strain. One patient with the disease repeatedly scolded me for not visiting him, although I was doing so on a daily basis! How much worse then for a wife, husband, son or daughter to have their compassion and concern apparently so quickly overlooked. Usually, most informed relatives understand and cope with this but in moments of tiredness it can cause great despair. Being unable to share their joys and frustrations with someone who has previously been so close often leads to a bottling up of emotions. When they are tired — and this can be a perpetual state for caregivers — they can lose their temper, which can then lead to guilty feelings.

As well as receiving little thanks for their efforts — acts of true unconditional love — relatives are also grieving for their lost loved one. But because he or she is still with them physically, the grief is confusing to them, and open expression is difficult. All these negative emotions have an impact on healing, both on the surface and deep in the body. They are the reason why support groups for families of Alzheimer's sufferers, and for other debilitating illnesses, are so vitally important.

As the researchers pointed out, it also means that doctors and dentists should be cautious in the timing of surgery. And we should ask patients about their role as caregivers if they are presenting with problems that are slow to heal.

∽

Receiving and giving

Our bodymind is delightfully selfish. It is concerned with our own welfare, our own survival. Symptoms such as pain and fatigue talk to us alone. They can't be heard by others, even our closest friends.

As it has our interests at heart, our bodymind tries to protect us, and save us from losing energy. Mothers, in particular, can be so busy tending to their children and families that they are at risk of ignoring their own needs. The messages of the body, such as minor headaches, then have to become stronger to get noticed.

Before long, a dedicated and unselfish mother can develop pains that even pills cannot shift. Often I see mothers who are breast-feeding with pains in their hands and wrists, a condition commonly known as carpal tunnel syndrome. In Chinese medicine the meridians, or energy circuits, which pass through the breasts, also run down through the arms and wrists to the hands. We use points on these meridians to treat these pains and also breast problems. The circuit is named the pericardium or *heart protector* meridian. There is no known connection in Western medicine.

If in addition to their nurturing roles women take on arduous, repetitive jobs, their bodies tend to respond in the appropriate places. Keyboard operators develop arm pains, and if the situation continues a serious chronic overuse syndrome will develop. Unlike men, many women work 24-hour days.

There are times when we, as parents, have to be reminded to look after ourselves. Airlines are conscious of this. Flight attendants, when demonstrating the emergency drill to passengers before take-off, always instruct parents to place oxygen masks over their own mouths before tending to their children. In an emergency, a mother's first thought is almost always for her child. Recently, a young woman, Judy, came to see me with severe chronic pain in her ankle. She told me her dramatic story.

❧

Judy's story

Judy's eight-year-old son was playing football outside their home. The ball ended up in the road and he dashed over to fetch it. A car came round the corner, knocking him over. A parent's worst nightmare. He lay still and unconscious as Judy, in a state of numb shock, ran as fast as she could towards him. She tripped on the kerb, injuring her ankle. She felt no pain, quickly getting to her feet again. Rushing over to her son, she saw he wasn't breathing and started to give him cardiopulmonary resuscitation — the kiss of life.

He began to breathe, and her son's life was saved.

As the ambulance officer secured him to the stretcher, he looked down at Judy's leg to see a sharp bone protruding through the skin just above her ankle — a compound fracture of the tibia. As she glanced down, she was overcome by the most excruciating pain. She collapsed to the ground, was given morphine, and taken to the hospital alongside her unconscious son.

After a few days in intensive care, the son's condition improved. He has since made a full recovery.

Judy, however, despite successful surgical 'pinning' of her fracture, continued to suffer severe pain for 18 months. She was treated with all manner of medications and techniques by many therapists, including myself. Her pain is easier, but, unfortunately, still there to this day.

Lessons learned from Judy

1. When we are in 'survival mode', our bodies 'kindly' do not interfere with matters of life and death. This is commonly called the 'fight or flight' reaction: when we need to focus intently on a major danger to us or to someone who depends on us.

2. When this pressure is off, symptoms often occur as if to make up for lost time. Have you ever noticed how that headache, or cold, starts at 6 p.m. on a Friday?

3. A mother's love is essential to our species' survival.

Learning to say 'no'

Judy was in a position where she couldn't say 'no'. Even in hindsight, she wouldn't have changed the events that saved her son's life. Many people find themselves in similar but less dramatic predicaments. The messages are coming in loud and clear from their *bodymind*, but they find themselves in situations controlled by others. Victoria's story brought this home to me.

Victoria's story

Victoria first came to see me three years ago with pains in her shoulders, arms, and the back of her head; she was feeling generally run down. She was married with a two-year-old son. As in most young families, both parents had to work to meet their financial commitments.

Victoria worked a 40-hour week as a switchboard operator at a large communications company. She was diligent, friendly and popular with all her work colleagues. She helped organise the work rosters, frequently filling in for others at weekends when her husband could look after their son.

Her symptoms of 'burn-out' had been gradually worsening over the previous 18 months. Recognising this, she had tried to cut down the extra hours she worked. However, competition in the telecommunications industry had led to staff redundancies, with longer hours and more pressure on all the staff.

Victoria felt trapped but continued to 'give her all' at work, and as a wife and mother at home. We talked about these issues, and we tried to help with acupuncture and massage to relieve her pain and fatigue.

She had become depressed and was sleeping poorly, so her doctor had started her on a small dose of anti-depressant medication. I taught her some simple breathing and meditation exercises that I, myself, had found useful. All these measures helped to a degree, but really only supported Victoria at this difficult time in her life.

Later on that year, just before Christmas, she awoke with another headache. This was not unusual; she had had a restless night with her son crying with earache. She felt somehow different, but Victoria carried on, going to work after giving her family breakfast and taking her son to childcare.

While at work her headache became more severe; her vision began to blur and later that morning she collapsed, unconscious. She started to convulse as the distressed staff called an ambulance. She was taken to hospital where a sub-arachnoid (brain) haemorrhage was diagnosed.*

Victoria recovered slowly, with some resulting weakness in her left arm and leg. Arterial scans showed there to be a weak-walled artery, called a 'berry aneurysm', which Victoria had inherited and which had ruptured causing bleeding into the brain. She had been lucky — about a third who suffer from sub-arachnoid haemorrhage die from the illness.

As she recovered, there was more encouraging news. The site of rupture could be protected from further damage by a highly skilled surgical technique that involved placing a small metal clip just below the weakness.

The operation was carried out some months later, and has been a complete success. I have seen Victoria several times since and have played a part in helping her regain strength.

Now back at work part-time, she has noticed a new attitude there, with her employers and her colleagues supporting her with true concern. Victoria, herself, has found profound meaning in the whole experience. She has a fresh outlook on life, worrying less and under-standing her own needs more.

In her own words: 'I have learned to value myself more and to say "no" more often.'

---

* Victoria's symptoms earlier in the year — the pains and fatigue — were not associated with her subsequent sub-arachnoid haemorrhage.

Lessons learned from Victoria

1. It is very difficult for conscientious employees to say 'no' at work, even though their bodies are giving them clear messages to conserve energy for themselves. Mothers of all ages are particularly at risk.

2. We, as a society, take life-threatening illnesses very seriously, often overlooking debilitating, but less dramatic conditions, such as depression and chronic pain.

3. Illnesses, as well as symptoms, can prove to have *meaning*, leading to profound changes for the better. This can occur not just in the life of the sufferer but in the lives of friends, family and workmates.

4. Modern medicine has evolved to a highly sophisticated level. Life-saving techniques, such as the neurosurgery performed on Victoria, can set the scene for deep levels of healing and personal growth.

5. Victoria, like many who have survived a life-threatening illness, now lives more in the present, worrying less about the past and future. The negative emotions of guilt, worry and fear are now less likely to take a hold.

In the words of William Blake:

> He who kisses the joy as it flies
> Lives in eternity's sunrise.

Stopping smoking — discovering buried messages

We all know about the harmful effects of smoking. The damage done by the repeated exposure of nicotine on our heart and blood vessels, of carcinogens on all our tissues, especially our lungs. Wounds are slower to heal. I have found that all healing arts, including acupuncture, are less effective for those who smoke.

I have been asked to assist many people over the years who were trying to quit smoking. I have observed that on stopping, the body grieves for its lost friend. Every cell cries out for this buddy who has always been there when times were tough, or were just getting that way. A few puffs would reduce the worries, ease the tension, make the sadness that little bit more bearable. A doctor I know started smoking again after 20 years when he felt intensely sad at the break-up of a relationship. He had not felt that way for many years, and the memory of the relief from a cigarette was as strong and seductive as ever.

In Chinese medicine the *lung qi*, or energy, supports the body much as a frame supports a tent. Without it we feel flat — a real sad sack. The lung is associated with grief; we wail and cry, and in many cultures the bereaved beat their chests at the news of the loss of loved ones.

Yet grief and sadness do not seem to be damaging to the body unless repressed. Method-trained actors, who work through changing their own emotional states as they 'live out' their roles, were studied by psychologists Dr Ann Futterman and Dr Margaret Kemeny.[12] They asked the actors to imagine they had been rejected for an important part. They found that during the time of intense sadness there was an increase in the number of 'natural killer cells' in the blood, and that they worked more efficiently. These killer cells are our first line of defence when our bodies are infected by viruses.

When the actors imagined the joy of landing the part, their bodies responded in a similar way. Laughter and tears, therefore, seem to be equally healing. Anger turned inwards, however, is damaging.

Men, in particular, have suffered illnesses because of cultural difficulties in expressing emotions. As a result, tension is internalised, damaging the body itself. The traditional soothers of emotions, alcohol and tobacco, do not seem to prevent this happening. Although there is good evidence that a glass of wine a day is beneficial, dependence on alcohol causes widespread havoc on the body. Rather than soothe our nerves, we become agitated and aggressive.

Although excessive smoking doesn't produce such destruction to society, it certainly plays games with the *bodymind*. Although providing an emotional crutch at times of need, it also seems to prevent the free expression of emotions. Rather than rant and rave, or even cry, our feelings are soothed before they are acknowledged. Through mechanisms that are far from clear, the effects of tension are driven inwards. Diseases are left to develop unhindered by the usual warning signs.

Maybe this deception can be understood by looking to other cultures and religions. The Latin word *spiritus* means both breath and spirit. The Hebrew *rua'*, the Aramaic *ru'a*, and the Arabic *ruh* can all be translated as 'breath', 'wind', 'air' or 'spirit'. In Christianity there is a profound link between the Holy Spirit, which infuses all life, and the breath.

Sogyal Rinpoche explains the Buddhist perspective on the breath in *The Tibetan Book of Living and Dying*:

> In Buddhism the breath, prana in Sanskrit, is said to be the 'vehicle of the mind' because it is the prana that makes our mind move. So when you calm the mind by working skilfully with the breath, you are simultaneously and automatically taming and training the mind.

With each breath, we receive millions of 'recycled' atoms from the universe, and 'look after them' in our bodies, before setting them free again over the next weeks and months. We inspire and we expire. We can go days without food, hours without drink, but barely minutes without breathing. In a life-threatening emergency, we establish an airway before anything else. Little wonder we pay such a high price for tampering with the purity of the breath. The breath of life.

When a heavy smoker quits, a 'Pandora's Box' full of emotions is often opened, with irritability, mood swings, appetite changes and general intense misery. It's as if all these feelings, blocked for so many years, come to the surface, spilling out in one chaotic mess.

Harry found himself in this position.

Harry's story

Harry was 52 and a successful businessman. He had single-handedly built up a chain of clothing stores at the fashionable end of the market. He had not only survived, but thrived in an industry that is notoriously fickle and highly competitive.

This had come at some cost. He had been married three times, and freely admitted that the long hours, the times away, and his ambitious drive had in the past meant he had neglected his wives and family. His new wife, Sue, was 38; she wanted a child, and a father to be around for her child. Harry's blood pressure was high, and he had started, somewhat reluctantly, to take anti-hypertensive medication on the advice of his doctor. He was, yet again, strongly advised to stop smoking.

Harry had smoked a packet a day since he was 18.

This time, though, his new wife was equally adamant. Sue was a non-smoker and extremely health conscious — power walking with weights and working out at the gym three times a week. Harry couldn't keep up with her, even when walking their dog. Also, Sue made it clear that if she was to become pregnant, there would be no smoking in her presence. So Harry decided to quit for good.

He tried to do everything right. They took off for a week's holiday in Fiji where Harry took up golf again after several years' gap. He first noticed tightness in his shoulders, and on returning to work the next week, he felt his 'whole body was poisoned'. He developed tight chest pains, which prompted him to see his doctor. He informed him that he had never felt so bad since following the orders of his wife and doctor. His doctor checked his heart and chest, diagnosed hyperventilation syndrome, and referred Harry to a physiotherapist specialising in breathing techniques. He also sent him to me for a course of acupuncture to ease his withdrawal symptoms.

A year has now passed, and Harry has been diligent with his exercises. He recognises that at times of stress, he and many in his business breathe shallowly and rapidly, holding their shoulders tightly up as if guarding their chests. He consciously now brings the breath 'down' into his belly when he notices this, and has more energy through the day.

It's still not easy though. Recently, while overseas for a month, his symptoms returned. But he is now more willing to receive help, and accept the reality that bad breathing habits build up over generations, and are endemic in the commercial world.

He is no longer taking blood pressure pills as his readings are normal. Sue has noticed a great change in Harry — an openness and contentment.

They are now expecting their first child.

Lessons learned from Harry

1. Focusing on the breath can produce marked changes to one's health.

2. Smoking is harmful to the body in many ways, both physically and emotionally.

3. Receiving the breath correctly, truly valuing it, can play a part in deeper levels of healing. It can make us, as males, reflect on the demands and expectations we place on ourselves.

4. A loving, supportive relationship with a sharing of goals and purpose makes the healing journey easier.

5. Changing the habits of a lifetime is not easy but it can be done. It's never too late to change.

~

Overcoming fear

I have had a close connection with cancer sufferers over the years. After working as a junior doctor on a cancer ward in North London soon after qualifying, I quickly found myself elevated to the role of on-call radiotherapy registrar at Middlesex Hospital in central London. This rather rapid rise was not, unfortunately, due to academic merit. Two senior registrars had tragically died within a few weeks of each other — one of an overdose of barbiturates, and the other of a brain haemorrhage. So I assumed responsibility for a huge area of North London.

We used to run clinics in several North London hospitals. Two doctors often had to see and assess about 70 cancer patients in one afternoon; I vividly remember one elderly man dying peacefully in the waiting area before I could see him.

In the mid-seventies, patients in general were not informed about their illnesses, especially those with cancer. Many of the senior doctors were adamant that it was better to keep them in the dark for fear of 'upsetting' them. One junior doctor friend was so incensed by the patronising attitude of his consultant that he took it upon himself to inform all the patients under his care of their illness and their prognosis! Although he delivered his news with the utmost sincerity, he did so with little subtlety or tact. Also, he did so in rapid sequence as he conducted his early morning ward round. I was doing a round in the next ward, and hearing the pandemonium, hastily rushed over to find out what was happening.

My friend, the nursing sister and the consultant were noisily engaged in an angry exchange of words in the sister's office. There was much acrimonious pointing of fingers, and waving of fists. Beyond this was the sound of distressed weeping from most of the patients in the ward with nurses doing their best to console them with hugs and hankies.

The contrast between this scene and the childhood cancer unit at Auckland Hospital couldn't have been more striking. And more welcome. Because of my experience, I was asked to help out on the unit soon after we arrived in New Zealand. Parents and families were fully informed and involved in support groups. Doctors, nurses, children and parents were happy to be on first-name terms. We were invited to their parties, their birthdays and their summer camps.

Chemotherapy and radiotherapy were successfully treating more types of childhood cancer, lymphoma and leukaemia. Bone marrow transplants were beginning to give some children with leukaemia real hope of a complete cure. As well as administering to the children on the ward, I performed a weekly theatre list injecting chemotherapy drugs into their spinal fluid, and taking bone marrow biopsies from their pelvic bones.

Later in general practice, I took a particular interest in patients with cancer. As many patients were elderly, I gained much experience, and deep satisfaction, from looking after the terminally ill. This led to my involvement with the North Shore Hospice, working to develop a comprehensive system of terminal care in the area in which I live.

There are no strict ground rules for someone to follow when diagnosed with cancer. No universally correct way to deal with the uncertainties, the confusion and the distress. Every person, once properly informed, must find their own way, and it is our job as friends and professionals to stand alongside them.

When I first met Chloe, I really wasn't sure how I could do this.

Chloe's story

I first met Chloe a year ago. She moved to Auckland from Wellington, pursuing her career and passion in interior design. At 37 and single, she felt she now needed a new direction in life — a break from her past. She told me, rather furtively, that she hadn't been too well lately and needed a doctor in the background, someone who wasn't going to push pills or give her a hard time.

She showed me a collection of greeting cards she had just designed — bright, original and fun. I ordered a couple of dozen. The original artwork of my favourite now adorns the wall of my waiting area. The cards were selling well, allowing her time to assess the new, larger market for her interior designing skills.

After 20 minutes, I asked her more directly about her health problems. She hesitated for a few seconds and then, with a brief sigh, began to tell me her story. She had started to get headaches and blurring of her sight about six months previously. Looking back, she hadn't felt right all of the previous year. There were times she had coughed up small flecks of blood. At other times she would feel nauseous and vomit for no obvious reason. She had seen her doctor, who sent her to the hospital eye clinic. They found evidence of pressure building up behind her eyes, and a computerised scan had shown two tumour masses in her brain. A scan of her chest also showed a tumour, which was confirmed as lung cancer after tissue sampling. It was thought likely that the brain tumours represented secondary spread from the lung.

Chloe stopped smoking and was given a special type of steroid to reduce swelling within the skull cavity. She had to stop taking this because of side effects. She did, however, have a course of 'palliative' radiation to her head which had thinned her hair. It was now growing back nicely.

At this point, I needed to find out what she wanted from me. 'Give me some orders, then,' I asked.

'No problem,' she said.

Order No. 1. 'I'd like a medical check-up, please.'

Order No. 2. 'Is there anything you can do to keep me healthy? I have just started these herbs. Are they any good? And what about acupuncture? Would that give me a boost?'

Order No. 3. 'And please never, never, treat me like a sick person.'

'What, never?'

She shook her head.

'Well,' I said, trembling slightly, 'I suppose the greater part of you is well.'

'You got it in one,' replied Chloe.

I felt I had passed the first test. Feeling a bit braver, I asked: 'Would it be possible . . . just a thought, mind you . . . for me to get your doctor in Wellington to fax over some more details?'

A long pause.

'Please, I did buy the cards.'

She laughed. 'Well, okay.'

Negotiations seemingly complete I set about trying to honour my side of the deal.

The faxed notes confirmed Chloe's story, together with her wishes not to discuss the future in medical terms. Her condition was incurable, and all they could offer was palliative care. They expected her to 'deteriorate severely in the near future'. On reading this, I knew I was going to be tested again soon. What happened if she developed symptoms I couldn't ignore? Could I order any tests? Was I being manipulated? Why did she need a doctor anyway?

I decided to take things step by step — one day at a time. We had arranged to meet again two weeks later. I wondered if she would turn up. She did.

She felt good and we started on some breathing exercises, enhanced by some gentle, relaxing acupuncture. We talked about how she could create an environment for healing on the deck of her rented flat. There was shade from a large pine, and she overlooked an expanse of bush. Chloe was also starting yoga, and was learning to watch the breath, and to sit still observing her thoughts. We practised this together.

We didn't mention her illness.

Two weeks later Chloe phoned weeping and distressed. She felt awful, headachy and nauseous. What did I think was happening? It was crunch time already. Fearing the pressure was building up in her head, I said that I really should see her that same day. She didn't turn up. She did phone two days later to tell me she was feeling better. She returned two weeks later looking the picture of health. This scene was repeated on two further occasions. One time, she had severe mouth ulcers. I explained that usually I would check a blood sample, but I suspected she would be unhappy with this. I was right.

I began to realise I was experiencing the same frustrations, the same sense of powerlessness Chloe and all cancer sufferers must feel. And that this contrasted starkly with the problem-solving mindset I had still deeply conditioned in me. But I was beginning to feel more comfortable in my role as supporter of the healthy side of Chloe. This was helped by Chloe's ability to bounce back to health after these short-lived relapses. She explained that she just tended to 'sit out' the bad times. It seemed to help talking to me, although she admitted to not always following my advice.

A little later, she came to see me to discuss another matter that had been preying on her mind. She confessed there were other reasons for moving to Auckland, apart from the career opportunities. She had been in love with someone here and wondered if she still felt the same. He was a leading lawyer and she had been deeply hurt through the relationship. I didn't pursue the details, as it seemed enough for me to know just this. It appeared he had been, and still was, married and living, in Chloe's words, a double life. She had arranged to meet him. What did I think?

I felt it was a good idea. Although it could prove difficult, it might help remove frustration and other emotional blocks to healing.

She returned to me soon after, telling me how it had gone. She said she now saw him in a new light. Despite his material wealth, he appeared empty. She sensed a lack of direction in his life, his fear and indecision. She knew she shouldn't see him again, she didn't need his problems; they were for him alone to resolve. And whereas before she had been experiencing a confusing, heady mix of love and anger, it now no longer seemed to matter. No more bitterness, no more regrets, only relief.

Chloe was also becoming aware of fear in others. She avoided reading the papers, and watching violent television programmes. News items especially upset her. She became uncomfortable in certain people's company, and went to extreme lengths to avoid them. She had already moved twice to escape landlords; both had drinking problems. In all, Chloe would move five times in the year.

A year has now passed. No blood tests. No X-rays. Chloe feels and looks well. Neither of us knows what lies ahead. At the moment of writing, she is heading for Sydney, to stay a while with friends and to try her luck in a bigger city.

Lessons learned from Chloe

1. There are many different ways to face a life-threatening illness. Honouring one's healthy persona and living life positively shouldn't be thought of as unusual. Chloe's request to be 'never treated as sick' was less a statement of denial, more an affirmation of life.

2. Our own roles, as good friends or as health professionals, are as much to do with supporting someone as they are with offering our advice and expertise.

3. Chloe, by confronting a previous painful relationship, released herself from the controlling grip of negative emotions. She was able to forgive while retaining her self-respect.

4. It is important to continue to follow our passions, tackle problems, and devise solutions despite our diagnosis and clinical predictions.

5. We should all honour our senses, feeding them with a healthy environment.

6. Until we are strong enough, it is all right to avoid completely a 'toxic' environment. This not only refers to cigarette smoke, pollution and unhealthy food; it means we can keep away from fearful, aggressive and draining people. We can say no.

7. We all have the potential to heal even when there is no cure.

With a little help from my friends — support groups

> What would you do if I sang out of tune?
> Would you stand up and walk out on me?
>
> LENNON/McCARTNEY

When your body goes out of tune, friends can be hard to find. Yet we know that social isolation is associated with delayed healing. Studies show that having a large number of social contacts actually protects a person from contracting the flu and other respiratory illnesses.[9] Married cancer patients have been shown to survive longer than those who are single.[13] Even more remarkably, support groups for cancer patients not only relieve the burden of the illness and the side effects of therapy, they have also been shown to increase the survival time of the members.

In the 1980s Dr David Spiegel at Stanford University conducted a landmark study into the beneficial impact of support groups on patients with chronic illnesses.[3] His findings have spurred further trials that have also observed the beneficial effects of social support, and 'structured psychiatric' intervention.[14, 15]

In Dr Spiegel's study 86 women with advanced breast cancer were divided into two groups, matched for the degree of cancer spread, age and marital status. Both groups continued to receive their routine medical care.

The intervention group — subdivided into three smaller groups — met for 90 minutes every week for a year. Facilitating each group was either a psychiatrist, Dr Spiegel, or a social worker with a therapist who had breast cancer in remission.

The sessions were structured with the following topics covered:

1. General coping skills; living as fully as possible.
2. Discussion of physical problems including side effects of chemo-therapy and radiation.

3. Self-hypnosis techniques for pain control.
4. Encouragement to express their feelings.
5. Encouragement to be more assertive with doctors.
6. How to extract meaning from their difficult situation.
7. How to help other patients and their families in the same situation.
8. How to improve communication with family members.
9. Facing and mastering fears about death and dying.

Both the researchers and the participants were unaware at the time that this intervention could affect their survival. The initial intention was to see if the groups could help reduce the symptoms of advanced breast cancer and its treatment. It was only when records of the survival times of the group members were studied 10 years later that it was discovered they had lived longer.

Whereas the control group, those not attending the therapy groups, lived for an average of 19 months from the start of the study, the intervention group survived for 37 months, almost twice the time.

So what actually happens in these groups to facilitate healing? We have already discussed the value of disclosure, of allowing people to relate their story in their own way. And the value of a listener in being able to make this happen. It is very common, in the midst of such a story, for a patient to pause and ask me: 'Are you sure you want to be bothered hearing all this?' Of course, I reassure them that most definitely it is okay.

In a group of fellow sufferers, this doubt disappears as so often the speaker is relating a story familiar to the others. Their attention is fixed on the person talking about problems so like their own, but often from a new angle with fresh insights. It is also my experience that group members form friendships that extend far beyond the group structure. They tend to meet socially, helping each other out when the need arises. Dr Spiegel describes the close bonds and friendships that developed between group members. He writes:

> The therapy group patients visited each other in hospital, wrote poems and even had a meeting at the home of a dying member.

Recently one group I brought together tactfully informed me, after only the third meeting, that they had decided to meet weekly at an upmarket café. It was to be midday on Tuesdays. They knew this would be impossible for me but they were sure they could cope without me. They still meet and by all accounts are making great progress.

When among such friends, there is no need for pretence. No need to make excuses for having a bad day or feeling muddled. There is also a direct honesty; the hard questions are asked and not easily dodged. A skilled facilitator can often play a part in making this happen.

In cancer support groups, there is also evidence that actually talking openly about dying in such a safe environment not only relieves unnecessary fears surrounding the dying process; it may also help lengthen survival times.[3] Those who fear death less, live more.

In my daily practice, I often act as matchmaker, introducing patients to others with similar symptoms so they can talk to each other about their coping strategies. Sometimes we have a consultation *à trois*, with myself acting as a go-between while at the same time picking up some marvellous tips I can pass on to others. Anyone feeling alone with a chronic illness should suggest this to his or her doctor. It always proves to be a rewarding experience.

I have helped run mindbody groups for a number of years. Here are some comments from the members of our current group, which has been meeting fortnightly for three years.

Jan, with chronic fatigue syndrome:

Sharing our life stories was a very powerful exercise. It not only bonded the members of the group, but also provided insight into possible causes as to how and why the whole person — mind, body, emotions and spirit — has become sick.

Brigitte, with rheumatoid arthritis:

Making those links with others on the journey and seeing the changes made — each in her own time, while supporting one another — all contribute to one's own healing.

Linda, with systemic lupus erythematosis:

For five very different people, who didn't know each other previously, we have built up understanding, empathy and support. I'm happy sharing things without being judged. We share laughs as well as bad times.

Diet

There are many excellent books on nutrition, which plays an essential role in healing. This is a subject I do not intend to cover in depth because so much good information is available elsewhere from authors with expertise beyond my own.

My own advice is quite simple. We receive the energy vital to life from two main sources: the air we breathe and the food we eat. When the body is unwell or under stress, we should pay careful attention to both.

When we are tired or unwell, we cannot be as welcoming for guests to our home. Our bodies too, when unwell, need to be careful what they admit inside. Most patients I see with chronic pain or fatigue are particularly sensitive to many food and environmental toxins. Their bodies are overloaded enough. So it is eminently sensible not to add to this.

It is particularly important to eliminate (or at least severely restrict) the following:

1. Nicotine.
2. Caffeine (coffee, tea), energy drinks, chocolate.
3. All unnecessary prescription and non-prescription drugs.
4. Preservatives, colouring and artificial flavours.

◆ Eat a balanced diet, as recommended by all nutritionists, with an emphasis on whole grain cereals, moderate carbohydrates and reduced saturated fat.
◆ Eat regularly and slowly. Remember that digestion begins in the mouth; so chew and taste. Don't think too much, worry or watch television while you eat. Just enjoy the food and the company.
◆ When chronically unwell, especially if the immune system is compromised, include a multi-vitamin compound with a balanced mixture of trace elements and anti-oxidants.
◆ Drink water frequently throughout the day.
◆ If you are concerned about specific food intolerances, try elimination diets — ideally under the guidance of a nutritionist.

In my experience, when the body settles back into healthy balance it can cope with a less strict regime.

Environmental pollution

Many of those consulting me wonder whether their symptoms are a direct result of exposure to an environmental toxin. Common concerns are around pesticides and herbicides — i.e., Roundup, paraquat, DDT, 245-T, etc. There is also much publicity about the effects of mercury in amalgam tooth fillings.

As with food toxicities, a body whose immune system is compromised may be more at risk from exposure to these chemicals. Because they add to the 'toxic load' they can further stress the system. People often get confused because they have been told this is the sole cause of their health problem. In my experience, the causes are not that simple.

Although I support, and often recommend, therapists involved in identifying and eliminating toxins, I see such work best done within the holistic context explained in this chapter.

Detoxification, often through homoeopathic means, can lead to a reduction of symptoms, allowing the person to tackle the other issues more effectively with renewed insight.

Electromagnetic stress

It seems very sensible for us all, healthy and not-so-healthy, to be aware of unseen hazards around us both at home and outside. All those whose immune systems are sensitive, i.e., the young or compromised, should be cautious about exposure to this potential hazard. This issue is vehemently debated at present, and I follow Hippocrates' advice of *primum non nocere* – first do no harm.

My work with acupuncture has brought me into contact with the enormous range of sensitivity shown in different human beings. Simply resting a tiny needle on one person's skin may produce a greater effect than acupuncturing 10 points in someone else. Our sensitivities change from hour to hour, minute to minute. Sometimes we get a sharp bolt of static electricity from our car; at other times not. So it makes sense to me to be cautious in this controversial area, and not to generalise, as I suspect some are more at risk than others. I therefore advise patients to read some of the excellent publications on the subject, or consult a practitioner who can come to the house with the necessary detection equipment and advice.

The changes recommended here are sensible for us all, in whatever state of health. However, the vast majority of people coming to me dream of a life some time without too many restrictions. They want to relax occasionally, eat the yummy things at their favourite restaurant, and not live in constant fear of being poisoned when they go outside. They want to live like everyone else.

Those who heal from a debilitating illness through their own will and means tend to be very sensible in their habits. They have learned along the way to value their health and respect their bodies. They often tend to favour organic foods, vegetarianism, animal and human rights. They see themselves at one with the world; at peace with their surroundings.

Maybe that is what it is, to be healed.

Clearing the way: a simple summary

1. Our bodies guide us to a state of healing. We can see our bodies' symptoms as messages, advising us about what is in our best interests. We can see our illnesses in the same light.
2. Repressed emotions have been shown to affect our health adversely. Bottling up emotions associated with stressful times in the past actually slows the healing process.
3. Telling your story the way you see it to someone, or a group, who listens has been shown to free up the body for healing.
4. Writing down an account of your story, and of past traumas, also promotes healing. Ponder over any 'meaning' you can derive from your story.
5. There is usually more than one reason why healing is blocked. Everybody's story is unique.
6. Grief may remain in a confused and unresolved state for years, even decades. It is never too late to derive benefit from grief counselling.
7. All levels of healing, even cuts and wounds, slow down when caring for a loved one in a stressful situation.
8. Our bodies carry on in rescue mode in an emergency, often 'giving out' after the crisis is over.
9. Saying 'no' before your body forces you to stop is difficult, especially for women in today's economic climate. Learning to receive as much as we give is essential to maintaining good health.
10. Smoking is an emotional crutch, which drives feelings inwards, thereby blocking healing. Your breath is precious. Stopping smoking

initially may open a Pandora's Box of emotions and uncomfortable symptoms, but it will also lead to healing and growth.

11. Learn to be assertive to doctors and healing professionals about your healthcare. Value your health above everything.

12. Be careful to time surgery sensibly, and be aware of how stresses, new and old, may hold up your recovery.

13. Find the environment you feel most at ease in. Avoid fearful or 'toxic' people.

14. Forgiveness frees up you, the forgiver. You deserve to let go.

15. Social isolation delays healing. You need to be with interested people. You will also help them enormously while you listen and learn. Ask your doctor to introduce you to people in a similar state. If you have a chronic illness, find out about local 'open' support groups or smaller mindbody therapy groups. If no one is running one, encourage your doctor or complementary practitioner to start one. If you have cancer, go to an established, professionally run group.

16. Avoid toxins. Eat sensibly, enjoying your food. If you are involved in detoxification and dietary programmes, approach your management in a truly holistic way.

17. Remember that your body is in a constant, dynamic state of healing.

Exercises

1. Write about the most stressful time(s) in your life
This applies to everyone, well or unwell. Take yourself back to the most difficult time in your life. If you can face it, write an account of it. Write it for *your eyes only*. Be as honest as you can with yourself.

Because relating the experience will frequently be a deeply emotional experience itself, don't worry if you get worked up, laugh or cry. When this happens, it is often a good sign.

If you have had many traumas in your life, write about one at a time. Only start the next account when you feel ready. You can leave it for days, or even weeks.

After doing this exercise, think about talking to your partner/spouse/friend about the tough times. It may be much easier now. Throw away, or shred the account if you wish. The exercise is designed to free you of past baggage.

Make a note of any beneficial effects — any improvement of mood, pain levels or fatigue.

Seek professional help if any issues arise that seem strange or slow to resolve.

2. Write your story

This is for those in less than 'perfect' health. Take yourself off to a quiet room. After a few minutes of recollection, start to write down your own story. You can use the stories in this chapter as a guide.

Start where you like. Mention the events, relationships and any other factors you feel are important — even if doctors and other health professionals have not taken notice of them. Don't worry about the grammar or spelling — this record is primarily for you. Instead write from the heart. Be creative if you wish. Draw pictures, compose poems or limericks. Take your time. Come back to it after a few days.

Show it to your spouse or partner only if you wish. Consider giving a copy to your family doctor. Ask him or her to read it and put it in your file. Bring a copy with you whenever you visit a doctor or holistic practitioner. If he or she is not interested, go elsewhere!

If you enjoy it, consider writing a daily journal.

3. Storytelling

If you have a chronic illness and find it tiring, or painful to write, find a trained listener. This could involve a counsellor, minister, nurse, doctor or health professional. Your local support group, church, or your local Citizens' Advice Bureau might help.

Feel comfortable you are being listened to, and not being hurried. Assure yourself that your story is to be kept strictly confidential.

4. Join a support group

(a) Open groups

Open groups are locally run groups for people with specific illnesses — e.g., Parkinson's disease, breast cancer, rheumatoid arthritis, epilepsy, etc. They are usually run by sufferers themselves. They tend to meet monthly for support and camaraderie. Frequently there is an invited speaker, who has some experience of the illness from an orthodox or complementary view. The attendance varies — usually 30–50 people if the topic is interesting.

Caregivers are usually welcome. With certain illnesses, especially Alzheimer's disease and other neurological conditions, there are support groups specifically for the caregivers.

See these support networks as a necessary part of your treatment. Remember, scientific studies show them to have healing effects of their very own.

(b) Closed groups

These are smaller, more structured groups often involving only 6–10 people. They are most successful if people are matched up by one of the facilitators. Just one misplaced person can upset the whole dynamics of a group.

Ask your doctor, or an 'open' support group about who to contact. Cancer sufferers should contact their local cancer society.

These groups have been shown to be remarkably beneficial to many.

However, they are not for everyone. If after one or two sessions you feel uncomfortable, talk to the facilitator. Go with your instincts.

Be reassured that everything discussed by the group is *strictly confidential*.

(c) Find a 'buddy'

If you have a rare chronic condition, ask your doctor if he or she has anyone like you in the practice. It doesn't matter if the conditions are not completely alike. Ask your doctor to be a matchmaker, acting within the privacy laws.

Consider joint consultations with your buddy and your doctor. This way you get double or triple the time for the same fee!

3. Mindful healing

We have now reached an understanding of some of the barriers to healing. Repressed feelings, and a lack of loving support, loom large as potential blocks. Blocks, once understood, can be cleared.

When we are sick, motivation can be a problem. Our confidence is often low, and even simple daily tasks prove difficult. Yet, we need to start to re-own our lives — new friends are great, but what can we do regularly, on a daily basis, to keep us on course?

This chapter is dedicated to learning simple tricks that lead to creating the right environment within us. But first, we must set out a simple goal, and work out what we hope to achieve.

Finding peace

Ask yourself: 'How much peace is there in my life?'

I always ask this when I am seeing someone for the first time. Chronic illnesses are chaotic and controlling. Even on good days there is little peace as we scramble around, fitting in as many chores as we can. No wonder we collapse in a heap. Then there are family responsibilities — how on earth can a mother of three children all under six achieve a sense of peace? And yet when we are well this is precisely our state — at peace with ourselves and the world.

Peace doesn't necessarily mean quiet inactivity. A peaceful protest can be noisy, musical or even humorous. We talk about peace and quiet as separate entities. Peace to a healthy teenager may differ from the peace yearned by an elderly, lonely widow.

Peace is valued from the cradle to the grave. A mother feeding a baby, either from the breast or bottle, is a calming, beautiful experience; two humans totally fulfilled with nothing else important on their minds. In a blissful setting like this, mother and child literally lose all sense of time. There is no place they would rather be. The peace that this special union creates flows on through the home to other family members.

I see this also in the homes of the dying. The overriding aim of palliative care is to help create a sense of peace in the terminally ill; when this is achieved, it can be shared around the entire family for years, dispelling fears of death, and keeping alive precious memories of a loved one.

Mindfulness

We all know this feeling. We are so wrapped up in what we are doing that time flies. We look at our watch and say, 'Heavens, is that the time?'

Humans worry. We shouldn't worry that we worry; a skilled defensive driver has to scan the road and pavements ahead constantly for potential dangers. It is our awareness and worry about the possible consequences that ultimately prevents such accidents. Where there is anticipation, and a highly evolved sense of self, there is also worry.

So we must come to terms with the fact that we are born worriers. But health requires balance. Too much worry blocks our quality of life. One way of rediscovering this is to allow others who seem free of these burdens to share their secrets with us. Also we should look closely at our own daily routines — how we eat and drink, for example — and ask ourselves whether simple pleasures have become hurried chores.

Who and what can help us become more mindful?

1. Children

As young children haven't yet learned basic survival skills, parents take on the worrying role for them. This is part of being a good parent. But we can in return learn much from young children.

They have little sense of time. Only 'right now' is important — their minds are wide open to absorb any experience, unhindered by our 'adult' tendency to analyse, and criticise.

It is a great joy and privilege for parents and grandparents to join children in their own private world of mindfulness. Playing, talking and laughing spontaneously, not afraid of what others may be thinking of them; children share these gifts with us unselfishly.

2. Animals

> There is no psychiatrist in the world like a puppy licking your face.
>
> ANON

Animals are also wonderful catalysts for a mindful state. By and large, pets are spontaneous and loving, and simply being in their presence calms, relaxes and heals. A horse and rider, like a mother and child, can be in a state of oneness as is evident during showjumping and dressage. The rider joins in the timeless state of the horse, involved in a less complex, but nonetheless real world.

Fish, so often seen in tanks in doctors' and dentists' waiting rooms, convey peace by the ease of their movements. Watching tropical fish can be an excellent aid to relaxation programmes.

3. Music

When we are listening to a familiar piece of music, we are engaging in a highly evolved process. As well as following the notes, absorbed in the present, we retain the memory of the melody we have just heard, while anticipating the flow of the music to come. We are thus mindfully in the moment, but at the same time comforted and secure in its familiarity. The composers of Baroque music had this in mind, and the works of Bach, Handel and Vivaldi survive to this day as perfect antidotes to daily stresses.

Of course, not all music relaxes. It can excite, seduce and energise us. We can still be lost mindfully in rock and roll, even heavy metal. Improvised jazz plays with our anticipation of melody and rhythm, often joining the artist and listener in a fascinating, creative partnership. It is, however, the softer, soothing rhythms that are best tolerated and most healing when we are feeling fragile.

4. Food

Many of us have forgotten the pleasures of mindful eating. Fast food, eating on the run, has become the normal habit for those with busy lives. Eating becomes relegated to a secondary activity, something we do while we're doing something else. We listen to the radio, scan the newspaper, watch TV, or even drive while swallowing huge chunks of food designed precisely for this purpose. Because we have no time to chew it properly, it has to be strongly spiced and flavoured for us to notice it. It fills the spot.

Exercise

Take one raisin, and place it in your mouth. Don't try to chew or swallow it, rather move it slowly around your mouth with your tongue, feeling its texture. Savour the taste of the solitary raisin, and focus your mind on it to the exclusion of all else. See how long you can extract flavour from this tiny morsel — try for 10 minutes.

This exercise is a useful introduction to the principles of meditation, with its focus on simplicity and *being*. It also highlights how unhealthy our eating habits have become; we are asking so much of our bodies to perform so many tasks at once. By eating quickly, with other business on our minds, we deliver poorly nutritious food to intestines that can't cope. Our digestive juices have no time to dissolve the food, and we absorb fats unselectively.

Mealtimes should be enjoyable, fun times. We should be involved in good-humoured, friendly banter, avoiding topics that require deep thought or invoke conflict. If we eat in this environment, we can even get away with a less than perfect diet.

By tasting mindfully, we rediscover that food is a special gift to the body. By respecting it, we honour one of our deepest needs.

5. Drink

Most of us struggle to keep our fluid intake up to an adequate level during our busy working days. We know that we should be drinking two litres, or eight glasses, of water a day but in practice most of us find this difficult. Keeping a plastic drinking bottle — the type professional sportspeople use — with you at all times seems to be an effective solution. Ensure your place of work and home has an adequate supply of cool, purified water for regular, fresh refills.

Take the time to *taste* the water. As with food, the more mindful we become with our drinking the less we need strong, artificial flavours. Children should be introduced to the joys of drinking water at an early age. Advertising and peer pressure will inevitably seduce them into drinking sweetened, flavoured and caffeinated products; but many parents are able to bring balance to this, with 'designer' drink bottles adorned with photos of their favourite TV stars.

Although healing is enhanced by eliminating caffeine and alcohol, most folk I see find these restrictions difficult. They yearn for the time they can live a life with the freedom enjoyed by their friends and family.

Even when they know they will suffer the next day, most will throw caution to the wind every now and then.

A compromise is to carry a water bottle at all times, alternating your drinks with polite 'swigs'. You should also drink slowly and mindfully. Approach wine as if you were a professional connoisseur, savouring the taste in different parts of your mouth — practise with the raisin. Drink only good wine. Similarly, drink beer or lager out of a small wine glass, again lingering over the taste. Choose the best beer and use your best glass.

6. Daily mindfulness

The pace of modern life and our many responsibilities prevent us from achieving the ultimate mindful state. But every day, we should set aside time we can lose track of. Having a bath, polishing silver, doing the dishes; just be absorbed in the task.

If you go for a swim, close your eyes, float and wallow. While out for a walk, focus just on the movement of your limbs. Try walking slowly and deliberately from your front door to your gate. If it's 10 metres, try to make it last three minutes.

It is difficult to be mindful watching television. Even when the programmes are not promoting tension and pain, sponsors' messages distract us, demanding our instant attention. Reading the newspaper, or even a good novel, is not truly mindful either. Making love is much better.

Breathing

Most of us have to relearn how to breathe. It is our most vital subconscious activity, and yet modern living conspires to interfere, conditioning us into bad breathing habits. I have come to recognise these traits in my own breathing patterns — possibly instilled into me on the parade ground as an air-force cadet at boarding school.

Chest out, stomach in is fine when we are involved in mortal combat; we protect our hearts as we fight or flee. But our modern battles are fought in the boardroom, in the parliamentary debating chamber, and on the stock-market floor. For many of us there is no let-up, as we move from one pressured situation to another. The computer age, with all its exciting advantages, has fed society's need for instant satisfaction. The cheque can no longer be in the post. Deadlines can no longer be staggered.

Nowhere is this more evident than in the offices of large legal firms.

As corporate legal battles are fiercely fought, it is not only the lawyers who are caught in the crossfire. Today's legal secretaries possess special qualities: they are efficient, protective, knowledgeable and nurturing. They prepare their employers for impending conflict, balancing military precision with true maternal compassion. They are also frequent visitors to my office, with neck and arm pains, and fatigue.

After listening to the all-too-familiar story, we talk about breathing. How easy it is to pick up someone else's breathing habit. I still find myself caught out by this.

As doctors, we see many people every day in tense and rushed states. Their breathing is shallow, and their speech pressured as they try to explain all between breaths. Automatically, we can find ourselves doing the same; matching them breath by breath. We don't want to appear off-hand, uncaring.

So we harmonise with them, and quickly catch their symptoms. Our shoulders become tight as we carry their load.

After a while the exchange is complete. They feel 'better already'. The tension in our own shoulders has spread. Our heads are banging and we feel weary.

There is a better way. When I find myself in this condition, I purposefully *re-position* my breath. Rather than catch their problem, I convert their energy into something useful, bringing the breath down to a place it can work for me. The tense person doesn't notice this or interpret it as a callous, uncaring act. They are too bound up in their own complex misfortunes.

I direct my breath to my navel — the umbilicus. This is where we receive our oxygen, and our nutrition when babies in the womb. Babies and young children are the best teachers of breathing. They continue to do it perfectly after birth. Watch how a healthy baby's abdomen expands

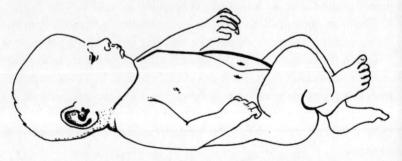

Abdomen moves upwards as baby breathes in

outwards during the in-breath, returning back effortlessly when breathing out.

The baby is relaxed and in *receiving* mode. In Chinese medicine, the umbilicus is sited on the *Conception Vessel* meridian on the softer (*yin*) surface of the body. Both 'receive' and 'conceive' are derived from the Latin *capere* — to take; so the gift of breath is *taken* down to this area. In contrast, the meridian running down the middle of our backs is called the *governor vessel* meridian, on our harder (*yang*) surface. A strong governor vessel keeps us upright and erect in a commanding military posture.

> He is the very picture of a modern Major General
>
> GILBERT AND SULLIVAN, *PIRATES OF PENZANCE*

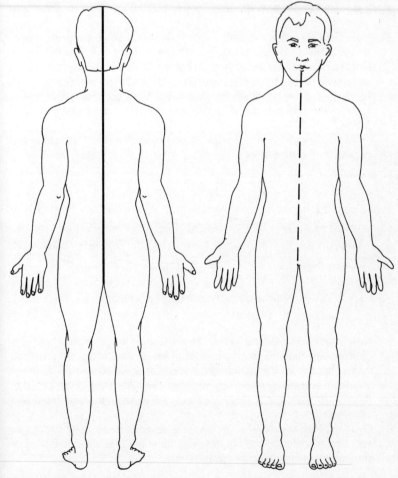

The Governor Vessel   The Conception Vessel

Breathing abdominally, like a baby, is now recognised in all cultures as the healthiest, most efficient way to receive air. It forms the basis of *yoga* in the Indian subcontinent, and of *qi-gong* and many of the martial arts in China and Japan. In the West, we refer to it as *diaphragmatic* breathing. The diaphragm is the membranous structure that marks the lower border of the lungs; it descends into the abdominal cavity as we breathe in.

Rather than trying to picture this anatomy, most people find it easier to visualise the breath travelling to a point *just under their navel*.

Exercises

1. Find a quiet spot to lie down.
2. Place one hand over your navel. As you breathe in, notice whether your hand rises or falls.
3. Now focus on gently expanding your abdomen as you breathe in, making sure your hand moves upwards towards the ceiling. Let your tummy return to its place of rest on breathing out. Practise this for a few minutes, gently and slowly. Try not to be cross with yourself if it doesn't seem easy.
4. Focus your attention down on your navel. With your hand still over it, visualise the breath being drawn to and 'feeding' an area beneath your palm.

   As you breathe out, just relax, noticing your hand and abdomen sink back to their resting place.

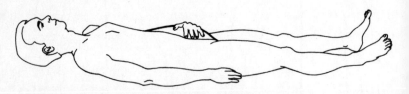

Feel the abdomen move up as you breathe

5. Now imagine that all the oxygen atoms you are breathing are specks of glitter — the type that stick when you throw a handful against a surface. As you breathe in, the sparkly glitter is drawn down to your navel, where it gathers and sticks. As you breathe out it remains there to be joined by more in the next breath. This visualisation will enhance the receiving quality of the exercise.
6. Smile! As with all exercises, this is to be enjoyed. It is important to cultivate your 'inner smile' — the one reserved for you alone. Keep it turned on throughout all breathing exercises.

Thich Nhat Hanh, the Vietnamese Buddhist monk who was nominated by Martin Luther King for the Nobel Peace prize, offers this simple exercise:

> Breathe in with the word 'calming' in your mind
> Breathe out with the word 'smiling' in your mind

Ten minutes' practice a day is all that is needed. If you can't set aside a special quiet time, do this before you go to sleep. Never try to force the breath, or over-breathe.

You will quickly recognise the times when you are breathing shallowly during the day. Rather than getting annoyed with yourself, bring the breath down gently to the navel.

You will also notice shallow breathing in others — at work, on the television and even on the radio. Consciously check your own breathing, reminding yourself not to catch their tension.

Gradually, with practice, this breathing will become sub-conscious — your normal, regular pattern. Friends will comment on your peaceful glow.

You may decide to progress to other, more complex exercises. I have found focusing on the positive, receiving qualities of good inspiratory breathing by far the most useful. As with all healing techniques, the simplest is the best.

Practising this exercise regularly has the following benefits:

◆ Improved energy, through more efficient oxygenation of the tissues.
◆ Reduction in headaches and painful necks: These muscles contract in tight spasms with the muscles of the chest when the body is defending itself against stress. This is the cause of tension headaches, and can contribute to migraines.
◆ Reduction of symptoms in heart and lung disease: The Chinese say that there is a stagnation, or blockage, of qi energy in the chest and upper body, which can contribute to heart and lung diseases. In Western terms, all patients with ischaemic heart disease, asthma and emphysema will benefit from this exercise.
◆ Appetite balance: When bored or unsatisfied, many turn to binge-eating for comfort. By rediscovering that the air we breathe, as well as the food we eat, is a satisfying gift, we can take comfort without expanding our waistlines. Air has no calories.
◆ Peace and balance: Research shows that a gentle, mindful focus on

breathing, whatever the exercise, promotes a balanced body chemistry — the ideal environment for healing. We focus on our very being, our immediate needs, our connection with our world.

Meditation

There are many different methods of meditative practice but all seek to achieve the same goal — a sense of peace and healing. In keeping with the aims of this book, I will describe simple exercises that are easy to learn, and can fit into our busy lives.

Meditation is not confined to any one religion. Nor is practising it a religious statement. In its broadest context, it is a pure state of mindfulness; a time when we can step outside our worries and fears. A place where we ourselves exist, unburdened and free.

Chronic illness adds a further load onto our system. Worries and fears can suck dry precious energy reserves. Meditation courses, although often excellent, require a commitment in time and money that many in this position find too difficult. In my experience, too rigid a structure sees many give up, disappointed and dejected.

There are no bad meditations.

Simply sitting in silence for 15 minutes a day, whatever happens at the time, is a valuable healing experience. Sometimes all that happens is an awareness of a spinning mind that carries on spinning. A worry that stays there. But just by allowing yourself to *be*, silently, not expecting yourself to come up with all the answers, you are valuing yourself above your problems.

When everything is going wrong, or you feel angry with yourself or someone else, sit quietly and observe your worries. Often they will mellow and settle as they do after a good sleep.

Meditation, however simple, can have a gradual but profound effect on your life. Rather than striving for a state of 'enlightenment', I prefer to encourage those beginning to meditate with a rather less dramatic but more attainable goal — 'self-awareness'. In Chapter 10, we explore how healing and this awareness of self are inextricably linked and why gaining a perspective on exactly where we fit in the world is so important.

Many people tell me they find the concept of meditation difficult. They have understood that it involves actively 'not thinking', and this has left them uncomfortable and concerned. They fear losing their edge, their sharpness and their reasoning. They may also be wary of mystical and

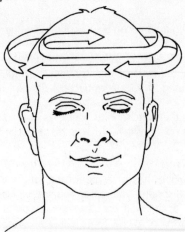

The spinning mind

religious overtones, although this causes far less concern than it did a decade ago.

I reply that as far as I know, it is impossible to block thoughts. Thoughts are our inspirations, our ideas. We have thousands of ideas every hour. They are fuel to our creativity; as Prospero remarked in *The Tempest*:

We are such stuff as dreams are made on . . .

We can, however, learn to be selective. It is because we have so many inspirations that we can't afford to have them blocked out by negative thoughts.

A batsman in cricket can only build a large innings by recognising not only the balls he must hit but those he must leave alone. When I let a negative thought go, I tell myself, 'Well left!'

Simple meditation exercise No. 1

1. The set-up
Find a quiet private place; disconnect or turn off your phone. Now choose a hard but comfortable chair — such as from the dining room or kitchen. Next choose a single flower in a small vase — or a candle — to be the focus of your attention. Place the object on a table or stool about two metres away from your chair. Take off any personal accessories you may be wearing. Smile.

2. The gaze

Sit comfortably with your hands on your thighs above the knee, and your spine fairly straight. Now gaze at the flower to the exclusion of all else. You may blink but do not divert your eyes. Allow everything else to become distant and blurred. After a few moments of this, try 'looking through' the flower, so it too becomes de-focused. If your eyes become dry and uncomfortable, close your eyes now.

You can continue the exercise with your eyes open or closed. Personally, I find keeping my eyes open more rewarding, but do what feels right for you.

3. Observe your thoughts

Don't try to stop thinking. Just be aware of the activity in your head. Release 'trains of thought'. As soon as you realise you are thinking a thought, release it. This allows room for the next one. As soon as you are aware of this new one, release it — and so on.

To begin with this isn't too easy. You will find yourself latching on; don't be cross with yourself, just instantly release and keep the inner smile!

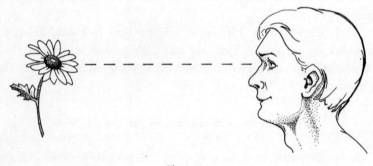

The gaze

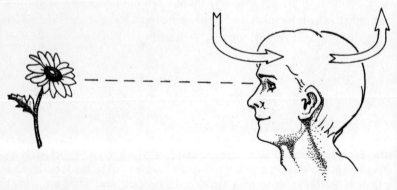

Observe your thoughts

This exercise begins by touching on our sense of belonging — our *universality* — in common with most healing rituals. Our breathing exercise followed this path with the visualisation of glitter representing oxygen atoms given unselfishly to us by plants. This time we have used our *sight* to lead us into this state of awareness. By allowing our sight to blur, we honour the continual nature of the universe, with atoms freely exchanged between living beings, as if we had no true boundaries.

So we become aware of ourselves as 'clusters' of recycled atoms in a dynamic state of balance with a universe of friendly atoms, all conspiring 'to make our day'.

Simple meditation exercise No. 2

1. The set-up
As before, find a quiet place and a hard chair to sit on. Turn off or disconnect your phone and take off any personal accessories.

2. Visualising
Close your eyes. Imagine that you are sitting beside a river, on a u-bend, with the water flowing from your left to your right side. Your thoughts are now logs that are carried, one by one, in quick succession by the flowing tide. The logs appear, come to meet you, then flow away disappearing to the right.

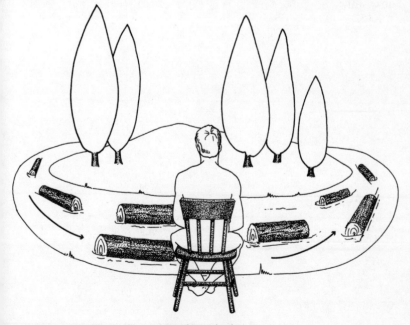

Watching the logs

As we sit watching the logs, we are passive observers. In real life, exercises such as this have an automatic, marked flow-on effect. We learn to go with the flow but because we have been selective, our heads are not crammed full of tiring and useless information. Far from losing our edge, we are receptive, on the ball, up with the play.

Creativity now has a chance to flourish. All these mindful rituals honour the receptive powers we all possess. As with our breath, we can use any sense to lead us into a mindful, meditative state — our taste, hearing, sight, touch and smell. Each time, we remind ourselves that we are simple living beings, unique but not alone.

Feel free to experiment and to mix-and-match. You will learn to combine the breathing and meditative exercises, and to use mini-versions while waiting for a bus or just before you line up that important putt.

Peace and stillness during meditation will develop with practice. You will reach a place outside your thoughts, within your own space. You may wish to join a meditative group, learn TM, or explore the many fascinating breathing techniques of yoga or *qi-gong*. Alternatively, you may decide that one of these simple exercises is all you need to achieve a better quality of life.

Do whatever feels the most comfortable. And remember to smile the inner smile.

4. Healing bonds

How others can help

What is a friend? A single soul dwelling in two bodies.

— ARISTOTLE

What can someone else do to help you heal? How can anyone, outside your skin, outside your symptoms, bring about a meaningful change to your state of health. Of course, your doctor can prescribe pills, correct chemical changes, perform surgery — using skills and knowledge that might even save your life. But there are limits to this approach. You may have a chronic condition that the very best modern medicine struggles to improve. Or your tests may all be normal but you continue to feel unwell.

Patients go to great lengths to seek out doctors with good 'bedside manners', even if doctors rarely see them in bed anymore. The growth of complementary medicine largely reflects our need to be cared for and listened to. And rather than this being some naïve, forlorn hope borne out of complete scientific ignorance — as some sceptics would proclaim — objective evidence now seems to support these intuitive hunches. A clear picture is emerging of the healing benefits of being listened to and being appreciated by true friends who care in an unconditional way.

So strong is this message that doctors are looking again at the nature of the bonds they form with patients. The areas we have been taught to regard as placebo have become a focus of study themselves. As I have moved towards healing (rather than curing) practices, understanding these connections has become a personal goal. I see any technique I use, whether it is prescribing medication, performing acupuncture, or listening intently, as an extension of these bonds.

Most natural therapists openly admit that their mode of treatment accounts for only a part of the overall healing effect. Thus, the homoeopathic remedy is strengthened by the bond built up between the therapist and patient. The acupuncture needle acts as a conducting link between the therapist, the patient, and the outside world.

Socrates put it this way:

> I said that the cure itself is a certain leaf, but in addition to the drug there is a certain charm, which if someone chants when he makes use of it, the medicine altogether restores him to health, but without the charm there is no profit from the leaf.

Enthusiasm, and belief in the remedy is also important. When a drug comes on the market, there is much hype. Until recently, we as doctors were regularly wined and dined by drug companies, while absorbing the latest information on their newest products. Pleasant memories would be evoked in us whenever we reached for our prescription pads; succulent tastes and aromas would be recalled (you may well have wondered about that little smile and that far-away look on your doctor's face). It has been shown that a doctor's enthusiasm for a medication can raise the initial placebo response from its usual 30–40 percent to 70–90 percent.[16] However, this only works until the initial enthusiasm wanes. Now many medications are marketed directly to the public with advertising campaigns strategically timed to rally continuing enthusiasm in both doctors and patients. We see this phenomenon at work with the multi-level marketing campaigns of natural health products and dietary supplements. Infectious group enthusiasm used to promote healing aids, but how many have been shown to have lasting benefits?

But can we do better than this? Can we go beyond the enthusiasm and hype, and invoke changes in patients' bodies that last?

So often, someone with a chronic illness travels from therapist to therapist, each time being rewarded by an initial improvement of symptoms which seems to correspond to the confidence of the current therapist. I continue to experience this myself; in an attempt to put patients in perspective about this, I explain the phenomenon as a matter of routine. This has been a dilemma for me as, on one level, it may have the effect of dampening down this spontaneous and encouraging enthusiasm. However, I am convinced that a gentle, more measured approach opens the door to deep healing. Like a true friendship, a healing relationship must be allowed to grow: confidence must build, and trust must be earned. A good friend sticks around.

The challenge

Often I am tested early on in a relationship. On one occasion, my computer had omitted a whole paragraph of a summary I had composed for the referring doctor of a new patient. This lady had previously suffered at the hands of doctors who had not listened to her, and on receiving a copy of the letter was very upset with me. The version 'doctored' by my computer read as if I was extremely off-hand about her pain and suffering. There ensued a lively confrontation with the letter being produced and held out in front of me. I defended myself, without great dignity, against her accusations of my being yet another unfeeling doctor, before seeing the letter and realising what had happened. My explanation of events sounded rather feeble and it was only when I recovered my original letter from my files that I was let off the hook. But this baptism by fire helped secure a lasting friendship, which has played an integral part in her deeper healing.

I now expect my commitment to a healing relationship to be put to the test in an uncomfortable way from time to time. From my experience, honesty and humility are valued above perfection and pride.

Professor Ian McWhinney of the University of Western Ontario, Canada, is dedicated to restoring the humanitarian approach to medicine. He suggests four reasons why it can prove so difficult to be a healer:[17]

1. To be a healer you have to be involved.
2. To be a healer you have to know the person.
3. To be a healer you have to listen.
4. To listen you have to know yourself.

We shall now explore how you can get the most out of a healing consultation. You may initially feel that there are occasions when the interaction is not too important. Having a flu shot, or a wound dressed, for example. But remember, everyone is a potential healer — and every time we meet someone, even in the supermarket aisle, we are involved in a mini-healing consultation. Whoever you are consulting, whether a clairvoyant or a neurologist, use this checklist:*

---

* Qualifications, academic expertise and experience are already assumed to be adequate.

The Therapist Scorecard

1. Am I being listened to?

Sogyal Rinpoche, the popular Buddhist master, describes the ideal listening state:

> Really to listen in the way that is meant by the masters is to let go utterly of ourselves, to let go of all the information, all the concepts, all the ideas, and all the prejudices our heads are stuffed with.

Like all ideals, it is something more often reached for rather than attained. Most of us are happy if the person at least tries; therefore, score first for *effort*, and then for *effect*.

Effort: 1–5   *Effect: 1–5*

2. Am I being informed?

This doesn't mean merely the presence of an informed consent document. Although these have become useful, and legally necessary in many cases, they are no substitute for an open intention to share information. Make it easy for your therapist, especially if pushed for time. If information doesn't seem to spill forth from his or her lips, ask if some time could be spent on this at the next consultation.

Effort: 1–5   *Effect: 1–5*

3. The internet test

Produce a wad of papers about your condition from the internet, and ask your healer if he is interested in reading them. Watch his eyes. Observe at the next consultation whether the documents are in exactly the same spot on his desk where he had placed them a week before. If so, point this out, gently and tactfully, maintaining eye contact throughout. It is probable that he really meant to look at them but forgot. If he says this, consider giving him a good mark for honesty. If he then goes on about the pressures of his job — fetching teenage daughters from parties at all hours of the night, no time for golf, etc. — give him a reprieve, but expect some action before your next appointment. Match compassion with practicality.

Effort: 1–5   *Effect: 1–5*   *Honesty: 1–5*

4. Is your healer confident?

When we are confident in any task, we can relax and be receptive to others. Quiet confidence is important in all healing arts — a mindful state away from fear and insecurity. This does not mean over-confidence, an inflated ego, or a gung-ho approach.

It is the confidence that comes of knowing one's self, warts and all. It is the confidence to say, 'I don't know but I'll look it up.'

If, in answer to your tricky question, your healer reaches for a book or journal with heady enthusiasm, that is good. If he has to look up every single query you make, that is not so good. Sometimes, when you ask your question, he will say, 'Excuse me,' and disappear furtively out of the room. Most likely he has a stack of books and an on-line computer in the other room — the distinctive dial-up buzzes and squeaks from the internet modem are a sure give-away. Unfortunately, surfing the internet is both time-consuming and addictive; he is likely to get side-tracked onto websites bearing little relevance to your own problems. So if you suspect this is going on, ask him to come clean and to jot down the web addresses, so you can conduct your own search at home. You will probably find you know them all already.

Confidence: 1–3   Time Management: 1–3

5. Humour

Humour is often cited as a vital ingredient of a healthy, long-term relationship. When we laugh together, we resonate instantly, honestly and irrationally. We expose our vulnerability to anyone present; for a moment there are no plans, no schemes, no words. Victor Borge once described laughter as 'the shortest distance between two people'.

The medical literature is short on laughs. Try entering 'laughter' into any medical internet search engine; you'll find it a sobering experience. Up comes paper after paper on 'pathological laughter' — the inappropriate expression of joy in the psychiatrically unstable!

Of course, healers must use humour appropriately. They shouldn't embarrass or belittle you or take advantage of their captive audience by reciting joke after joke. A light-hearted, spontaneous air is all that is required.

As Ovid advised: 'To be loved, be lovable.'

Humour: 1–5

Although I have taken a whimsical look at the healer/patient relationship, I have tried to convey the essence of a deep-healing partnership. And despite this having neither the intensity nor the significance of a marriage or life partnership, parallels can be drawn. Early healing responses may be enhanced by enthusiasm and hope, much like when we first fall in love. But the passion and excitement of young love is gradually replaced by a deeper, more meaningful bond. An unconditional friendship which transcends the good times and the bad.

But can such subjective concepts as love, compassion and commitment be measured and evaluated? Does, or should, science play a part in unravelling these deep mysteries?

❧

Human/machine interactions

For 18 years, a complex research programme has been in progress addressing precisely these issues. Trying to measure the hitherto immeasurable. Scientists refer to such research as *anomalous* — deviating from the normal. The results so far from the Princeton Engineering Anomalies Research (PEAR) programme have been remarkable; if continuing research confirms their provisional findings, the implications for healing in the twenty-first century are far-reaching.

The programme, under the guidance of Professor Robert Jahn, examines how the human mind interacts with simple machines.[18] The machines used come in a variety of forms but all produce information in a random form — much like the machines that select numbers for a national lottery. The operators sit in front of the machines, known as Random Event Generators (REGs), but are unable to touch or in any way interfere with them physically. Through intention only, they try to change the 'output' of their machines using mind power — i.e., they try to will the results up or down, first recording their pre-stated intentions.

Over the years there have been over 100 operators, from all walks of life. None of these has claimed extraordinary powers before or after the experiments, had any special training, or received financial compensation. Over 50 million such interactions have been recorded, with more than three billion bits of binary information analysed. From this huge amount of data, intriguing patterns are emerging. These can be summarised as follows:

1. There is strong statistical evidence that, when averaged out, the output of the machines changes in line with the 'pre-stated intention' of the operators. In fact, the likelihood of these being chance findings has been calculated as being about one in a billion.
2. The pattern of these changes is recorded consistently throughout the group. When it comes to these mind games, it seems there are no superstars or dummies.
3. Certain individuals have identifiable 'trademark' effects on the machines. However, when they combine in pairs, a totally different 'signature' emerges. Male/female pairs do better than single-sex pairs. Males and females in a relationship do best of all.
4. No prior experience is necessary. In fact, the first set of experiments tended to produce the strongest correlation. The performances were then apt to wane, only to pick up subsequently.

This pattern may well be familiar to you. It is reminiscent of the placebo response we linked to 'enthusiasm' earlier in this chapter. Those who have experienced a course of acupuncture, or another healing art, may also recognise this pattern. It may even lend scientific insight into what we call 'beginner's luck'. All this is remarkable enough. However, it doesn't end here.

5. Statistically similar results were obtained when the operators addressed their machines from a distance of thousands of miles. The transfer of information between the operators and their machines was independent of distance.
6. Statistically similar results were obtained even when the machines were in their 'off' mode. So when the operators 'communicated' with the machines several hours before or after they were producing their data, the results were the same. This suggests that the transfer of information was independent of time.
7. Subjectively, the most successful operators reported a special coherent bond with their machines. A feeling of oneness, a resonance.

So what value is all this to those of us interested in healing, and how we humans relate to each other? Can we draw parallels?

We are already familiar with the notion of symptoms as information.

Messages within our bodies, giving signals to us vital for our healing. We have already seen themes emerging common to both individual healing journeys and respected research — for example, the value of honest, compassionate relationships. In humans, researchers have measured blood cells, lung function tests, pain scores, and even survival times in an attempt to evaluate the effects of these bonds.

Nevertheless, orthodox medical science has not yet attempted to define or come to terms with these connections; its focus has been on influencing the body from within. We will explore reasons behind this in Chapter 7, which takes us on a journey from this 'closed' view of curing to an 'open' view of healing. In turn, this leads us to scientific theories on the make-up of information fields, and how they relate to our very consciousness.

Meanwhile, we can extract many clues from the PEAR research. Our bodies are information systems millions of times more complex than the machines used in this series of experiments — no computer can yet match the storage power of a single cell. Just as man and machine have been shown to bond, we begin to see parallels with our own human, interpersonal experiences. The importance of noble intentions, and 'tuning in' to people by listening without judgement. Why a loving relationship can survive time and great distances between partners. It may even begin to explain phenomena hitherto referred to as para-normal — for example, remote, extrasensory perception.

Whatever it shows us, it certainly appears to be an important piece of the healing jigsaw; one that seems to lock neatly into another intriguing area of research — the scientific investigation of prayer.

Prayer

A *Time*/CNN survey in June 1996 revealed that 82 percent of Americans believed in the 'healing power of personal prayer' and 73 percent believed that 'praying for someone else can help cure their illness'. So Western culture, it seems, believes prayer has an important part to play in health, despite the apparent separation of medicine from spiritual issues over the past 300 years.

More than half of the 130 scientific papers on prayer reach the same conclusion. Heart surgery patients, one recent study has shown, left hospital on average two days earlier if they were assigned chaplains. This represented a cost saving of about $US4200 for each patient.[19]

A 1988 study of 393 coronary care patients in San Francisco divided people into two groups: those prayed for, and those not.[20] Each person was assigned a distant '*pray-er*' but was not informed about this.

The 'pray-er' was given a photograph of the patient to pray for and the progress of all trial patients was followed for 10 months. The prayed-for group required five times less antibiotics, and were three times less likely to develop heart failure. None required artificial airways intubation, compared with 12 of the 'non-prayed-for' group.

The literature on 'therapeutic prayer' covers all the world's major religions; in general, emphasis is placed on spiritual practice rather than religious affiliation. Like the Princeton research, it provides strong evidence for a mind/consciousness that transcends the boundaries of orthodox medicine's view of the brain.

Dr Larry Dossey, the author of several books on the subject, has conducted extensive research on the effects of prayer and the power of the mind.[21] He questions the prevailing, limited view of a mind locked into a brain:

> The brain can't wander around; it's located in a specific place. The mind, however, can wander. Yet scientists argue that your mind is the same as your brain. It's the guiding belief in modern science. Prayer research shows the mind is more than the brain. I don't know any study that shows the brain can affect someone on the other side of the earth. Clearly the mind can do it through prayer.

This year at our national medical acupuncture conference, we decided to make use of this research. One session was devoted to putting our collective minds to the unfortunate plight of a patient with severe pain and fatigue symptoms. Her doctor presented her case, hoping for some guidance from the group of 50 doctors and physiotherapists. After an hour of discussing and debating her case, we decided to hold a minute's silence for her, when we focused our thoughts and good intentions on her. We later reflected, rather ironically, on how this is still an accepted practice for remembrance of the dead; somehow the living seemed to have been forgotten along the way.

A few weeks later, I mentioned our ritual to a friend, a heart specialist. I suggested that it could be a good idea for this to happen at the next international cardiology convention he attended.

'Imagine the healing power of 500 eminent world experts,' I suggested flatteringly. (I purposefully omitted the 'no superstar' evidence.)

He seemed interested. I noticed him take a small calculator out of his wallet.

'Now,' he said, 'let's see. A minute, you say. So we divide my hourly charge-out rate in dollars by 60, multiply that by 500 . . .'

His deadpan face dissolved into a broad smile. He was joking of course . . . I think.

5. Healing and dying

> After several weeks, grumbling in the congregation made it clear that death troubled him to a greater degree than it did them. Many thought it not the tragedy Monroe did, but saw it rather as a good thing. They were looking forward to the rest.
>
> — CHARLES FRAZIER, *COLD MOUNTAIN*

Doctors and patients can talk at cross-purposes. As a newly qualified doctor, death seemed a long way off for me. I was 23, in love and trained to save lives. I loved the idea of being alive. I still do. I suspect in those days I was, like the evangelical Reverend Monroe in *Cold Mountain*, guilty of imparting my own agenda on the gravely ill. Not with stern, tedious sermons, I hope, but with the silent assumption that death carried with it a universal stamp of dread and fear.

My experience with terminally ill adult cancer patients in London did little to help. Junior doctors, by and large, were not trained to talk of death. And patients, by and large, seldom asked. The dying were prescribed cocktails of heroin, major tranquillisers, and cocaine in ever-increasing doses; no doubt a compassionate attempt by us to help drown the sorrows of terminal illness. The hospice and palliative care movement was then in its infancy. With its growth, the needs of the dying are now being honoured and understood; drugs are used for specific symptoms, such as pain and nausea, rather than to produce an 'altered-state' of euphoria. In those days, the dying process was kept under a veil of secrecy, concealed from both patient and doctor.

And so it was until my first real teachers arrived; the children of Ward 32, Princess Mary Hospital, Auckland. Children with cancer. Rangi, a

10-year-old Maori boy with a rare form of leukaemia, stands out vividly in my memory. Rangi told it like it was.

'Are you pregnant or just fat?' he asked a senior nurse the day he was admitted for tests. Thankfully she was the former.

A day later he spied a visiting father, an amputee, leaving the ward.

'Hey you, mister,' shouted Rangi up the crowded corridor, 'how come you got one arm then?'

Rangi was not one to bow easily to authority. But he endured transfusions, bone marrow biopsies and endless blood tests without a tear. One day I overheard him talking to his mother.

'Are you going to be okay Mum? Dying's all right, you know.'

No one had told Rangi he was dying. In fact, we were striving against the odds towards a remission of his illness. But Rangi was right; the chemotherapy was not working and he lived for just one more week.

On many occasions since, I have witnessed terminally ill children teaching their parents and families about matters of life and death. I have seen families and communities heal, unite and forgive under their simple, guiding wisdom. Parents who were alcoholic, and drug addicts, start to reform their lives. Children have shown me how healing can occur through the dying process; and why adults frequently find it so difficult to let go of life.

Letting go

As children we had less trouble letting go. If we were lucky enough to be surrounded by a loving family, it is likely we weren't constantly tense or worried. A young child may be ill one moment and full of life the next; this embarrassing transformation usually occurs the moment you carry your child into your doctor's office.

Children rarely bear grudges, worry about their reputations, or procrastinate. It is so easy to lose the simple pleasures of our childhood as we struggle to gain security by accumulating material wealth. For some, possessions become the main focus of their lives, continually trying to grasp at power in the fear of letting it slip. However, in the process more precious commodities slip by: joy, values, spontaneity, and some would say wisdom.

It is perfectly normal for the dying to go through a phase of agitation before reaching peace. Jobs need to be finished, wills checked, friends and relatives seen — the pressure is on. At times, old scores need to be settled. It is so often a time of forgiveness, of healing old wounds. Those whose pleasures in life have been exclusively materialistic tend to have the most trouble letting go. Tension, irritability, insomnia result as a battle rages within. A forlorn battle to retain control of a situation where wealth matters little. All that can be perceived is loss and failure. Doctors may struggle with large doses of morphine and tranquillisers to control symptoms borne out of years of repressed and hidden feelings.

Once the dying person has let go, a peaceful calm follows. This late stage can, in turn, have a wonderfully soothing effect on those privileged enough to be present. I have felt the most relaxed in my life sitting alongside the bed of a dying person — no need to talk or plan, no better place to be. And one's own relaxed, meditative state is truly palliative to the dying.

Agitation in the final days of life can result from the tension and fear of a family member. On one such occasion, I noticed a dying man's son in an agitated state by the bedside. The patient had been restless, drifting in and out of a coma, unable to settle for days. I took the young man to a private room a short distance away from his father, leaving his mother and sister at the bedside. On closing the door he broke down and wept in grief. After a short while we returned to the room. All was now peaceful; his mother hugged her son, saying that all the tension had 'miraculously' left his father five minutes before. He died half an hour later.

Guide to visiting the dying

◆ *Treat the person exactly as you usually do. Be yourself. Be spontaneous.*

◆ *Talk about the issues of the day. The present is still important to the dying, despite this being a time of reflection.*

◆ *If he or she is resting, sit quietly and soak up the peace.*

◆ *Respect the dying person's right to solitude, if this is his or her wish.*

◆ *It is not disrespectful to smile or laugh. This can relax both of you.*

◆ *If near a window, comment on the day, and nature. Make sure there are healthy flowers or plants in the room.*

◆ *Practise your breathing or meditation, especially if the dying person is agitated. Both of you will gain much from this.*

◆ *Value each moment together. Treat each as a precious gift.*

Only a mother knows

Isabel's story

While working as a doctor in the hospice, I was called to see an elderly, widowed lady in the hospital nearby. She had advanced cancer and had started to have frequent epileptic fits four or five times a day. She had undergone brain scans as secondary tumours were suspected to be the cause. Surprisingly, though, the scans were clear.

The hospital staff had tried to control these fits with a variety of anti-convulsant medications, at increasing doses, but to no avail. To make matters worse, the nurses reported that she had become increasingly withdrawn and depressed. She was eating little and was unwilling to let them know if she was in pain. She wouldn't even talk to her children or grandchildren.

I visited her with Mata, a cancer specialist who had made her home in New Zealand with her husband, having to leave her grown-up children and family in Bosnia soon after the war there. Mata was battling the authorities so she could become registered as a doctor in her new country; meanwhile she was working as a volunteer, and as my valued advisor, at the hospice.

We entered the hospital room and I sat down beside the bed, offering my hand to the lady. As she looked up, ignoring my hand she fixed her gaze on Mata. I introduced myself, asking her if I could call her by her first name, Isabel. No reply was offered as she continued to look in Mata's direction.

'Hello,' said Mata, smiling. Isabel's gaze softened slightly.

I tried again. 'We're here to try to help.'

She turned her eyes towards me. 'What would you know? Only a mother knows.'

Her eyes then fixed firmly back onto Mata, who although still smiling, was now tearful.

We sat in silence for some time. I was happy to wait, if only to show Isabel we were still interested. After five minutes, I asked if it was all right if we came back some time. Isabel shrugged, and we left.

Outside, I asked Mata what she had meant. Her eyes, only just dried, became dewy again. 'A mother gives to her children all her life. It is her role, the expression of her love, the meaning in her life. Sometimes when this is taken away, we can feel we are left with nothing. Kindness, especially from someone who may remind Isabel of her own son, only serves to remind her what she can't do anymore. She wants to give, not take, love.'

Now we were both rather tearful. A concerned nurse asked us if we were all right, possibly wondering how experienced we were in our jobs.

We thought for a moment. 'Let's go back in,' I said. 'I think Isabel needs to hear that.'

With some gentle persuasion, Mata agreed. This time I stood in the corner by the door as Mata shared her insights with Isabel. Close enough, though, to see Isabel shed her own tears. She even looked my way and smiled. We said we would come back and see her in a couple of days. We advised the medical staff that we weren't adding in any new drugs.

Two days later, I was phoned by the charge nurse. Isabel had just died. 'But she had no more fits, and since you both visited there was a great change in her. She talked, even joked with us. Her family were so grateful.'

❧

Getting used to being on the receiving end of care and attention can prove difficult for many. This is particularly true with women and those whose lives have been dedicated to serving others. The thoughtfulness of most dying people continues to astound me — not wanting to be a burden, making sure those left behind are provided for. We have already seen what influence receiving love has on healing. A diagnosis of a life-threatening or chronic condition often brings with it a reappraisal of exactly what is important in life — how important each day is, being able to say no, to receive and give back. These are the affirmations of so many cancer sufferers, who discover new meaning to their lives after the initial feelings of shock and despair.

Men also have reputations and responsibilities in life which prepare them poorly for the helplessness of a terminal illness. The traditional role of breadwinner and even fixit-man can leave a man feeling inadequate when he can't fix himself. Men stay away from doctors, often until it's too late, for this very reason. We have tended to have difficulty expressing our true feelings.

Jack, an 82-year-old war veteran, had an even greater barrier to letting us in on his suffering; a stroke the previous year had left him *aphasic*. He knew what he wanted to say but was unable to get the words out.

It even took me days to discover that Jack wasn't his real name.

Jack's story

Jack's stroke had a big impact on his life. He felt isolated. Many of his good friends had died while those left behind either lacked the patience to wait while he struggled with his words or were too deaf to hear him. Sometimes his words wouldn't come at all.

The stroke had also left Jack weak and lame; he disliked having to use a stick to get around, remembering how hard he could work as a young man. During the Great Depression of the thirties he cultivated a large dairy farm in the North Island; he could neither afford, nor wish for, days off. By the time World War II broke out and he was called up, he was able to leave the running of the farm to his staff. His wife was expecting their first child, and took on the role of manager when he was posted overseas.

Jack captained a platoon in Greece. One day they were ambushed, suffering heavy losses. In fact, only Jack survived. Over the years he never talked about it even to his wife and family. They had never seen him cry about anything. But he had always been there for them; nothing was too much trouble.

After the war he carried on farming, became a councillor and supported the local Catholic church. However, his family noticed him lose interest in religion and confidence in his faith following his stroke.

Jack was admitted to the hospice as he had also been discovered to have an advanced cancer. Despite being given large doses of morphine, he was extremely restless. His weakness had meant that words were few and far between. He would be continually grimacing with no one able to discover whether this indicated severe pain, or indeed anything else. His wife and family were desperate for help.

At first we tried to adjust the doses of his medications. Often this is successful, but unfortunately not in Jack's case. I learned about Jack's life from talking alone with his wife. The hard work, the horrors of war, the testing of his faith, and his deep sense of duty.

I decided to relay Jack's own story back to him, hoping it would spark some recognition in him. I had wondered whether the anguish and feelings of guilt about his war experiences were now haunting him after years of repression. In fact, I put this to him directly, waiting a full 10 minutes for a reply.

'It's . . . not . . . Jack . . .' This was all he could say.

His wife visited that evening. I reported my slow progress, asking her why he would say that he wasn't Jack.

'Jack was in fact born "Harry",' she told me. 'His mother's brother, Jack, died a war hero at Gallipoli when my husband was only two. They changed Harry's name to Jack in his honour and insisted he kept this name in remembrance of his uncle.'

We both went back to 'Jack's' bedside. I recounted what I had just heard back to him. Jack, or rather Harry, started to cry, hugging his wife as tightly as he could. She had never seen him cry like this — not once in the 65 years they had known each other.

From that point on, his restlessness and grimacing stopped. He managed to smile, and even laugh, and we were able to reduce some of his medication. Two days later he summoned his parish priest to his bedside, asking him to conduct a simple ceremony reconfirming his faith.

He died peacefully the following day.

I have thought of Jack many times since. Did he finally recognise what a heavy cross he'd had to bear all his life, living up to the memory of his war-hero uncle? Had he finally buried the guilt and grief of losing his mates in the war, not far from where his uncle had fallen years before? Had all this been compounded by the frustration and embarrassments that his illnesses had brought?

I suppose all that really matters is that 'Jack' had somehow, and eventually, found peace and that his family could remember him, to the end, as a man of great kindness and dignity.

≈

Near-death experiences

Most people die peacefully. The many documented cases of Near Death Experiences (NDEs) now give us some clue about the subjective experience of dying. Of course, we can't assume this tells us the whole story; it is rather like having to predict the outcome of a football match from the score at halftime. However, reports of NDEs show a remarkable consistency: a gentle time of reflection, freedom and feelings of pure love.

There is also a body of evidence that shows us how important it is for people who have NDEs to be taken seriously.[22] I have been surprised how many patients have had such experiences in the past, often in hospital. Most have felt uncomfortable about relaying their stories to health professionals for fear of being ridiculed. But it is clear that when listened to and taken seriously, NDEs can be powerful catalysts to deep healing. It is an experience well worth recounting in the manner shown in Chapter 2. This can be done many years after the event because the memories remain fresh. As such, it is prudent to work closely with a modern health professional with whom the person can feel valued and secure.

> *Francesca found herself in the outside lane of the motorway. To her left, travelling at the same speed, was a huge truck with wheels almost as high as her small hatchback. The truck began to move out towards her; another car was close on her tail, and there was no space ahead. The median barrier was to her right. There was a crunch and a shudder; the truck driver hardly felt it but turned to see Francesca's squashed little car still moving, apparently stuck to the truck's side. He veered sharply back to his original lane, and amid screeching and horns pulled over to the verge.*
>
> *Francesca meanwhile ground to a halt in the fast lane, where she stayed until the traffic police got to her. Miraculously the following traffic somehow managed to avoid colliding into her rear.*
>
> *She came to me several days later with pains down her left side. She recounted the accident to me in detail.*
>
> *'You must have been scared stiff,' I remarked.*
>
> *'Well, that's the odd thing,' she replied. 'In fact, I have never felt so calm in all my life. I had no fear — just a relaxed peaceful state somehow removed from the pressures of my life. I seemed to be instantly aware of all the joys I have encountered in my life and how wonderful it's all been.*
>
> *She went on. 'But, it hasn't stopped there. Despite my pain, since the accident I seem to have become more intuitive, more spiritually aware. It's difficult to explain. It's as if I have my life more in perspective. I can now see the big picture.'*

Two days later, a different truck driver arrived at my rooms. He too had been in an accident. His truck had rolled, trapping him in his seat, leaving him in intensive care with serious chest injuries and continuous pain. A big, solid man who one would imagine not to be prone to flights of fancy.

'As I sat there, I felt no pain for a few moments. It was great . . . I didn't mind what happened. I saw myself stuck in the truck, as if I was outside looking in. I . . . became aware of Ben, my little boy who I see at weekends. Then I got this pain . . . I must have passed out. Next thing I remember was waking up in the hospital. I think I know what's important now.'

6. Healing, curing and childhood cancer

Seventy percent of all children with cancer can now be cured. Modern medicine has advanced and evolved to a point where many cancers no longer carry with them a death sentence. There is also real commitment from cancer specialists for treatment protocols such as chemotherapy and radiotherapy to become less toxic and more gentle.

It is understandable, therefore, that many cancer specialists are truly concerned when patients, especially children, forsake orthodox therapy in favour of alternative therapies. In New Zealand in 1999, the parents of a three-year-old boy, Liam Williams-Holloway, with cancer (neuroblastoma) abandoned chemotherapy because of the overwhelming side effects, despite the doctors' prognosis of a possible cure from such treatment. They turned instead to 'unproven alternative' therapy, which included treatment with a machine known as a Quantum Booster. The family disappeared, literally 'on the run', prompting the hospital authorities to go to court to declare the child a ward of the state.

The case received huge media interest. Popular opinion sided with the family, who received the overwhelming support of their local community. Eventually a media blackout was enforced in the interest of the child's health and the family's peace.

During this time I talked to many diverse groups about the family's dilemma — patients with cancer, cancer specialists, surgeons, and parents. We discussed it in our mindbody groups. All, like the parents of this boy, were informed, interested, caring people.

Again, I felt Liam was teaching us all a valuable lesson. As a parent I tried to place myself in his parents' position; how would I react to watching my child suffer as a result of the side effects of this powerful treatment?

The crying, the hair loss, the nausea. How much would this conflict with my own instincts to protect my child from the toxic effects of the world? Who would I really be doing this for? How much was this to do with my own fear of dying? Is death really the end? Most religions say no. Who really knows?

These are questions born out of love. I came to realise that in such a situation a parent's love could feel suffocated, compressed with fear. I would feel the need to escape with my child from this prison to a place of hope, compassion and healing. I would wonder what the atmosphere of fear was doing to my child and the family.

There is, I'm sure, a better way. Healing and curing are different. Complementary and interdependent but still different. There needs to be no fight between their advocates — they are not in competition. There is no room for egos. The compassion and true friendship of cancer support groups not only improves lives, but also lengthens them. Anything that compromises or interferes with loving relationships must be bad medicine.

Fear of dying must not dominate over the love of living.

I am unsure of just what my wife and I would do if faced with Liam's parents' awesome responsibilities. From the start, though, we would wish for the following from our medical and nursing staff:

1. That the doctors listen to our philosophies of life, our spiritual beliefs, our passions and our fears;
2. That together we share aims by identifying the healing needs of our child, and work out a programme that honours these needs;
3. That we would expect the medical and nursing team to understand the difference between healing and curing. That open communication should exist between any complementary healers and the medical and nursing team;
4. That we would protect our child against fear and be able to voice our concerns openly if a 'fearful' situation arose.

We would wish for the following from our natural therapists:

1. That they also understand the difference between healing and curing;

2. That their treatments honour the principles of healing with its focus on love and compassion, not on our fear of losing our child. True hope not false hope.

In this way, it would seem possible for the best of healing to co-exist with the best of curing. It may lead to the need for less toxic treatment and shorter cycles of chemotherapy and radiotherapy. It may even save lives.

7. Informed healing — understanding the bodymind

When we visit our doctor or dentist, we now expect to be fully informed about the medication prescribed or procedure performed. Although healing techniques are classically safe, the same standards should apply. We need to develop a deeper understanding of our *bodymind*.

Most of us have some knowledge of our own body's anatomy and chemistry. However, until recently the conventional view has been of a mind sitting in the brain, somehow separate from the body. Using this model, many would remark that the healing journeys already described would have occurred because of 'psychological', rather than 'physical' reasons.

However, as the stories, studies and exercises described so far strongly suggest, we are not simply isolated islands of human tissue closed off to the outside world. Healing involves interchange between ourselves, others and our environment; we are part of an *open system*. This challenges the very basis of the traditional, twentieth century health-care model, which sees our bodies as *closed* systems manipulated back to health from within. Medical science has progressed by studying each small part in increasing detail, with the assumption that this reductionist approach will provide us with all our answers.

This section deals with evidence, both new and old, that supports a more holistic, open model. A new picture of the body is emerging, with the mind itself an integral part of this — a broader image of the mind, viewed with a broader mind.

I believe that an understanding of these principles is in itself an important healing step. It allows a person seeking healing an opportunity to be involved, and thereby take responsibility for his or her healing. It also opens patients up to receiving the messages from their bodies, thereby gaining perspective and control of their health.

Some modern scientific evidence supports this approach, strongly suggesting that our minds exist within and throughout our bodies. We have already explored some evidence that our minds are capable of 'wandering' further than this; it seems humans can affect the output of machines at a distance. Prayer, it appears, can produce measurable changes in our bodies.

For the healing actions and intent of others to affect us, we also need to look closely at our *sensitivity*. How we perceive and receive messages from the outside world with our five known senses — and *extra-sensorily*.

It is this open model of healing that forms the basis of Chinese medicine. The Chinese have studied the body in this way for thousands of years; it is their insights that have helped me reach a deeper understanding of healing. They have provided us with a working model of healing.

You will see how closely their philosophies fit with the artistic vision of writers and poets from Western and Eastern cultures over the ages. Creative people who have intuitively explored the links between the body, the soul and the natural world.

The inner connections — the mind in the body

What is mind? No matter. What is matter? Never mind.

THOMAS HEWITT-KEY, 1799–1875

Everything we have discussed so far suggests that our bodies are part of our intelligence system. We seem to be more than intelligent heads attached to mobile heart-lung machines. Emotions and symptoms are our warning signs, protecting us, telling us to wise up. Our brain receives and sorts out this information — the computer modem and the terminal making sense of the messages coming in from the body's cyberspace. So just as there is far more to the internet than the computer on our desk, there is more to the mind than the brain.

Every day someone asks me: 'Do you think it's in the mind?'

'Well yes,' I say, predicting a deflated look on the person's face, swiftly adding, 'but the mind is in every part of the body.'

At this point, deflation turns to confusion — a definite step-up, but I realise further explanations are needed. I can list endless personal anecdotes, refer to the time-honoured wisdom of the Chinese, Indians and Native Americans, and even quote poets and authors. But for the hard evidence, for solid reinforcement, I prefer to turn to science.

And so, it was with a heady mix of relief, comfort and joy that I listened to two eminent and respected scientists explain their work uncovering evidence for this bodymind internet. Candace Pert and Michael Ruff are molecular scientists at Georgetown University, Washington DC. Professor Pert was the first scientist to prove the existence of a receptor site for morphine-like substances (opioids) on the surface of cells. This was a considerable scientific breakthrough in the early 1970s. This pioneering work was driven by the pharmaceutical industry, as it provided more proof that drugs work by somehow attaching themselves to our cell surfaces at specific sites.

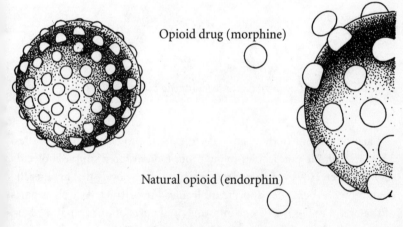

Opioid drug (morphine)

Natural opioid (endorphin)

Cells with receptor sites for molecules

In fact, it was work on the mood-altering drugs that confirmed that these sites can be linked to our feelings and emotions. When we feel down, we feel it in our bodies — our shoulders slump, we lose the spring in our step, we get that sinking feeling. When anxious, our heart races, our palms sweat, we tremble. Research over the past 30 years has uncovered over 80 chemicals — peptides — that respond to different emotional states and exert their influence on our cells by attaching themselves at these sites. Tranquillisers, such as valium, act by blocking the effects of these chemicals, by competing with them for these sites. Viruses, such as those responsible for HIV, also compete. Much research is underway trying to create a chemical that can stop the AIDS virus attaching to cell surfaces, from where it exerts its destructive influence. We are, therefore, seeing viruses, peptides and drugs competing against each other on the surface of our cells. Already we have a picture that begins to make sense of our life experiences.

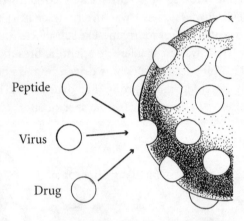

Competition for receptor site on cell wall

Each cell in our body is littered with many thousands of these sites. They are complex molecules many times larger than a simple molecule such as water. However, there are some parts of the body that are literally teeming with these sites and the molecules they attract. As well as parts of the brain, the lining of our intestines and parts of our spinal cord are particularly rich in what Candace Pert has termed 'molecules of emotion'. As well as validating those *gut* feelings, Professor Pert speculates on the meaning of this finding: [23]

> The anatomical distribution pattern of neuropeptides and their
> receptor sites — being enriched in several 'nodal points', like the dorsal
> horn of the spinal cord and other sensory input areas — suggests that
> all sensations and perceptions are filtered through our emotions.

This model suggests we have a thinking, conscious mind working with a subconscious mind throughout the body. This latter mind carries with it the memory of all that has gone before, as well as constantly informing and advising us. And just as we can get blocks in our conscious mind — writer's block, forgetting names, etc. — so we can get emotional blocks in our subconscious bodymind. These may manifest as pain, fatigue, constipation — all real, all physical. And it happens in all of us; there should be no cause for blame or accusations of not coping. It is, quite simply, the human condition.

Instant connections everywhere

The new picture emerging is that this type of 'emotional' information can pass from cell to cell in a way most of us will find difficult to believe. Doctors have been trained to 'see' the messages of the body as passing neatly along nerves which come to and fro from the brain. But the mindbody internet does not fit into this system of telegraph wires.[24] In fact, it appears that every cell can inform and work in with every other in the body — and it has to be remembered that there are about 60 trillion of them. Guts talking to skin, toes talking to heads. Clusters of these chemicals may coincide with 'zones of information' whose borders overlap our known anatomical borders. In future we may see these chemical clusters coincide with the mindbody zones described over centuries by Eastern physicians — the meridian and chakra systems with their holistic mindbody associations.

There is also speculation that this information travels instantly irrespective of distance. We have already seen this phenomenon in action outside the body in the Princeton PEAR experiments. There, researchers found that those participants who had a close, loving relationship with their machines seemed to have a freer flow of information with them, and that operators who had close interpersonal relationships with each other fared even better.

The lessons we have learned so far — that loving relationships with others and *with ourselves* are vital to healing — are now beginning to gain the scientific credence many of us need. Maybe we are seeing the end of the expression, 'So it's all in the head'.

The dance of the molecules

It appears that once a peptide molecule attaches itself to the surface of a cell at its receptor site, it transmits its message to the cell by vibrating — dancing a jig. In the following visualisation, I want you to behave like this molecule. Instead of finding a site out of thousands on the surface of a tiny cell, you are at an open air rock concert in search of a patch of ground to put your rug.

The rock concert — Visualisation Part 1

You arrive at the concert on a brilliantly fine day. The field is already packed with thousands of fans. You see a space, and make your way towards it determined to bag it before anyone else sees it.

Before long, there appears on stage your favourite band. They start their set with a rock and roll number — a few people, scattered around the crowd, stand up immediately and dance. Then more. The group sitting next to you get to their feet, then, despite being tired, you too can't resist the urge. You look around — everybody is up — dancing to the rhythm. All together, instantly linked by the music.

You are now in a helicopter above the concert (in a visualisation, like a dream, you can do anything!). You look down and see everybody dancing together in perfect harmony. You can't hear the music though.

Explanation

1. Our emotions can have a similar effect on our body, our cells, as music has on a crowd of rock fans. Emotions are like the music of the body providing an instant connection within our body.

2. Music affects us emotionally in an individual way. We can be profoundly moved by music. As T. S. Eliot explained in 'The Dry Salvages':

   > ... music heard so deeply
   > That it is not heard at all, but you are the music
   > While the music lasts.

3. The helicopter pilot can see the effects of the music — everyone dancing — but not hear the music itself. Similarly, a scientist can look down a microscope, or view a scan, but will see only one aspect, or dimension, of a greater whole. The molecules of emotion are not the emotions themselves.

The outer connections

The stories throughout this book reveal that healing involves more than just the mechanical repair of the body. Once healed, a world previously denied opens up. Opportunities present themselves, relationships improve, as a new focus develops on the outside world. The healed have an improved 'sense of self', often better than before the illness. In retrospect the illness gains new meaning; a means to a good end. So reconnecting with the environment is a vital aspect of healing. It is intrinsically woven into the process.

We connect with this world through our senses. Our sense organs pick up messages all the time, relaying them so that our bodies can make the necessary adjustments. We can also use these routes to good effect to enhance the process: a massage to the skin, music to the ears, aromas to the nose.

I would like to examine these outer connections from several angles, starting with the prevailing biomedical model, which I have been taught formally as a doctor. I will then extend this model into areas practising doctors can no longer ignore; the effects of 'hidden' forces on our bodies. We will also discover that to start to explain emotions we will have to broaden our vision to examine more experimental areas of science.

Temperature, touch and pain

Human beings are warm-blooded mammals. Unlike lizards, tortoises and dinosaurs, we have in-built mechanisms to ensure that although it's 5°C outside, our temperature inside stays around 36.8°C.

We do not have lizards' tough protective scaly skin. Instead, we have automatic self-regulating systems that monitor outside conditions; we come equipped with our very own thermostat. Before we are born, as we rest in our mother's womb, this apparatus has yet to function properly. There is no need since our mothers are doing it for us. If we arrive too early, we have to be placed in an artificial 'womb' or incubator, with an internal temperature as stable as our mother's. A preterm baby in an incubator is like a tortoise with a hard, transparent shell.

Our skin receives messages of touch, temperature and even the wind blowing. Without our conscious control, messages are passed along nerves to the spine, where some pass up to the subconscious brain, which in turn relays messages back down the spine and to the body as a whole via chemicals. As a result, a balanced, stable environment remains in the body.

If heat messages are sent, then chemicals are produced to expand or dilate blood vessels releasing heat in a manner similar to when we loosen our clothing. Sweat glands are activated that produce liquid to evaporate on our skin, thereby cooling us. If we are cold, the blood vessels contract, preserving warmth, and we get goose-bumps where our hairs stand up, trapping an insulating layer of air. We create our own woolly jumper.

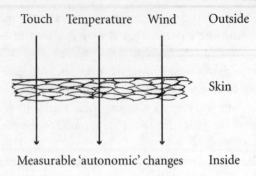

This is a function of our *autonomic nervous system*; its job is to keep us autonomous or independent by allowing our bodily functions to proceed without us having to worry about them 'consciously'.

Pain messages have a similar journey. Some of these travel to the conscious areas of the brain so we can respond, taking avoiding action; others are involved in reflex loops to and from the spine. They also set in motion endorphins and other chemicals which reduce the level of pain and start a whole cascade of chemical reactions that promote healing. This happens when we experience a 'jogger's high'.

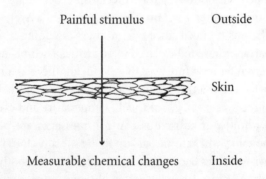

In reality, there are many interconnections being discovered between these pathways with many factors regulating and interfering with the system. We have already seen how chemicals, because of emotional experiences, can cluster around the spinal cord, helping explain why past events and traumas can disrupt the body's pain and regulating systems.

The autonomic system receives messages not just from the skin but from all our other senses. We can get goose-bumps from hearing Luciano Pavarotti singing 'Nessum Dorma'; we can also be physically aroused by erotic images. Smells can either whet our appetite or make us feel like vomiting. The autonomic nervous system, by relaying information from the outside world to our inside world, can be seen to have its own innate intelligence.

It allows us to relate to the world while at the same time helping allow our physical bodies to keep as stable and balanced as possible. It makes a major contribution to our sense of self. It recognises what is good and not so good for us, helping our bodies adapt and gently informing us of what is happening. It is our own in-built healer.

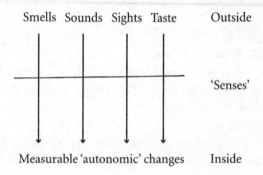

The immune system — deciding who's who

In addition, our autonomic nervous system is now known to link directly to our immune system. Lymph nodes, the thymus, and the spleen are supplied directly by autonomic nerves; a far cry from the teaching I received at medical school that depicted the immune system as working solely in isolation, neutralising and disposing of unwanted invaders such as bacteria and viruses. We can now extend this image to fit our more holistic model, which envisages the immune system having a role that contributes to and helps define our sense of self.

It acts like a bouncer at a party. It identifies unwanted, rowdy gate-crashers and evicts them. The bouncer has to have some intelligence. If he picks on honoured, invited guests, he will upset the whole party. He has to recognise who's who. Conditions such as rheumatoid arthritis and ulcerative colitis are examples of auto-immune conditions where precisely this scene is played out. The body has difficulty in recognising its own tissue, its own self.

To recap, we are now seeing models, accepted by doctors, that start to explain some of the healing patterns we have talked about. We now have a valid, proven model to explain how therapies such as massage and acupuncture can access our healing via our sense of touch. We can extend this to music therapy via our hearing, aromatherapy via smell, and even colour therapy via our sight. In my experience, many doctors are still sceptical about these areas, especially colour therapy. Yet I suspect few would put someone suffering from a severe migraine attack into a room where the walls were painted bright red!

As it is, our bodies can also change in response to forces undetected by our five senses.

Light — more than meets the eye

The sun's rays can turn our skin brown without our conscious awareness. Sunlight on our skin is a vital factor in making Vitamin D effective. People deprived of sunlight develop the deforming bone disease rickets.

We now know that exposure to the correct amount of light is important for the balanced production of melatonin from the pineal gland in our brains. Half an hour of sunlight (avoiding burns) during the day, and subdued lighting at night, seems to be ideal. International travel is one modern activity that upsets this balance. A related condition is Seasonal Affective Disorder, where those deprived of sunlight during northern winters develop symptoms of depression.

The tuatara lizard, a living relic from the Mesozoic Age, has a pineal gland (or third eye) uncovered by scales in its first six months of life. One major problem when trying to breed these lizards in artificial conditions has been the development of severe forms of calcium deficiency in the first year of their lives. Recent research by curator Lindsay Hazley at the world's only captive breeding programme of tuataras at Invercargill Museum, New Zealand, suggests that this condition can be prevented when the lizards are placed under ultraviolet light.

Until recently, it was assumed that the pineal glands of mammals and humans were only activated by messages received from the back of our eyes (the retinae). However, it is now known that migrating birds, with their thinner skulls, have pineal glands that are *directly* affected by light. There is also speculation about whether this occurs in human newborn babies as their skulls are thinner with open fontanelles — the 'soft' spots at the top of the head. As a young baby in England, I was placed in my pram outside for half an hour a day, come rain or shine, summer or winter. Interestingly, the practice was commonplace in the 1950s but is now rare.

Is there evidence that our bodies respond to light shone directly on our skin? A recent study at Cornell University challenges the belief that we receive light from our retinae alone.[25] Light was directed only to the skin behind the knee of human subjects, and measurements were made of the hormone melatonin and body temperature. Remarkably, the light was shown to have a direct effect on both these levels, suggesting that our skin is also a light-sensing organ.

If further studies confirm these findings, many healing therapies previously dismissed by mainstream medicine may begin to be validated. Infra-red lasers — infra-red exists in frequencies just outside the visible spectrum — have been used for several years as an alternative to needle acupuncture. In France, acupuncturists have detected changes in the wrist pulse when torchlight is shone on different areas of the skin. Colour therapy has been used for centuries in India. The door is now open for researchers to investigate how different wavelengths of light can aid healing.

The Cornell University study should herald a shift in mainstream thinking. By continuing to dismiss light and colour therapy out of hand, we could be denying people safe, effective drug-free treatment for insomnia, depression and many other imbalances.

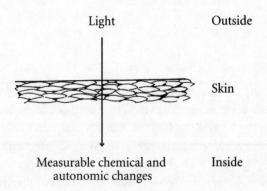

Light   Outside

Skin

Measurable chemical and   Inside
autonomic changes

Radiation

Light is only one type of electromagnetic radiation that passes into our bodies. Radiation can be both clinically effective as in the treatment of cancer or dangerous as in nuclear fallout.

The debate about the possible harmful effects of electromagnetic fields continues to rage. How dangerous are our cell phones, our microwave ovens, and high voltage wires? This is not only a scientific debate. It involves commercial self-interest, politics, and intractable belief systems. What is not in dispute is that these fields do pervade our bodies; what harm they do has yet to be 'proven' to the satisfaction of orthodox medicine. Medical authorities are beginning to advise caution in these areas, on the premise of 'first do no harm'. We, as yet, don't know if different age groups or people with certain illnesses are more at risk. Informed mothers are protecting their children, aware of these issues. Battles continue to be fought around the world whenever telecommunication companies plan transmitting station sites beside schools.

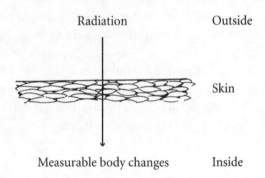

Sensitivity

Nothing in my medical training prepared me for the extreme range of sensitivity I now see in my daily work. For me, this was the most startling revelation when I started to practise acupuncture. After only a few days, I witnessed extraordinary variations in response to inserting a tiny needle into different people. Some turned green at the very suggestion. There were others, however, who were dramatically freed of pain the instant I inserted a needle just one millimetre under their skin at the site of a known acupuncture point. Not all would respond this way; most painful

Getting real with Albert Einstein

There are many ways of perceiving 'reality'. Our eyes receive light, but light occupies only one tiny band of frequencies in the whole electromagnetic spectrum. The twentieth century began with Albert Einstein broadening our understanding of the first Law of Thermodynamics which stated: 'Matter and energy cannot be created or destroyed, only converted from one form to another.'

Einstein's famous equation, $e = mc^2$, showed that energy (e) and mass (m) were interchangeable with the connecting link being a constant related to the speed of light (c).* From then on we were permitted to regard our bodies as either physical mass, or matter or energy. What we saw with our eyes, or felt with our touch, represented one small, albeit valid, part of reality. Mathematicians and scientists showed us precisely where visible light 'sat' within the whole electromagnetic spectrum.

Type	Frequency (Hz)
e.l.f. waves	less than 10
radio waves	$10^2 - 10^7$
micro waves	$10^7 - 10^{12}$
infra red	$10^{12} - 10^{15}$
visible light	10^{15} (only)
ultraviolet	$10^{15} - 10^{18}$
X-rays	$10^{18} - 10^{21}$
gamma waves	more than 10^{21}

conditions took longer, especially if they had been there for several weeks. And there was a group of about 15 percent of patients who failed to respond at all, despite having the same Western diagnosis as the others.

Children are, by nature, sensitive, open, enquiring and vulnerable. Their immune systems mirror this mercurial state; up one moment, down the next. They are, in general, extremely sensitive to gentle massage, therapeutic touch, and delicate acupuncture.

---

* This constant remains so because it comprises the 'frequency' of the waves, and the 'distance' between the peaks. The more frequent the waves, the smaller the distance between them.

I have also witnessed the same phenomenon in many adults. In my experience, sensitivity is particularly marked in:

◆ Pregnant women;
◆ Artistic and creative people;
◆ People with multiple sensitivities to food and medications;
◆ Many in chronic pain, particularly post-operative pain;
◆ Those who have had a life-threatening illness or near-death experience;
◆ Those undergoing practices enhancing self-awareness, i.e., meditation;
◆ The dying.

At present, because sensitivity is not measurable, orthodox medicine largely ignores this issue. When hypersensitivity to allergens is discovered in a patient, treatment has two main focuses. First, contact with the offending substance (e.g., penicillin, peanuts, dust mites, etc.) is avoided wherever possible. Secondly, the body is *desensitised* either through medication or by exposing the body to slowly increasing doses of the substance under the close eye of a doctor.

Although these are important and often life-saving measures, they fail to address the core issues of sensitivity. Sensitivity is still often seen as a weakness, rather than a strength. And rather than honour the sensitive, we try to recondition them into the 'normal' range. By failing to recognise people's innate sensitivity, we continue to be poor at predicting adverse reactions to drugs and surgical procedures. As ever, those suffering from conditions such as Chronic Fatigue Syndrome, Occupational Overuse Syndrome, and multiple chemical sensitivity will continue to be marginalised in our community. It also means that children whose sensitivity is dishonoured, or abused, may suffer throughout their lives. They may never reach their creative potential, or discover their true selves.

One example of human sensitivity that has been measured scientifically concerns the Chinese practice of applying the warming herb moxa to the little toes of pregnant women carrying breech babies. According to tradition, warming the outer corner of the mother's toe near the corner of the nail results in the baby moving, often to the head down position. Delivering the baby head first avoids potential complications and interventions such as the use of forceps or even Caesarean section. Until recently, this strange practice had not been put to the test under controlled conditions.

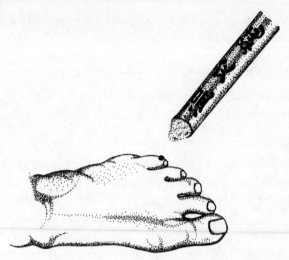

A burning moxa stick warming acupuncture point BL 67

In November 1998 the prestigious *Journal of the American Medical Association* (JAMA) published a trial that supports these observations.[26] Dr Francesco Cardini, from Milan, joined forces with Dr Huang Weixin, conducting research at two hospitals in China. Moxa heat was applied in the manner described, to the little toes of 130 women carrying breech babies in the thirty-third week of their first pregnancy. They were first shown the technique in the hospital outpatient clinic, then went home, performing it for 15 minutes to each foot once a day for a week. If the baby was still breech after this, they carried on for another week. An equal number of women with breech presentation were chosen as 'controls'. They received routine care but no 'moxibustion'.

Women in the treated group reported 37 percent more movements than those in the control group. What's more, 75 percent of the babies turned to head-first compared with 48 percent of the controls; they remained that way until delivery. The procedure known as external cephalic version — turning the baby round manually by manipulating the baby through the mother's abdominal wall — was used on some of the mothers in the control group. Even so, only 62 percent of babies in this group had turned by delivery day.

I have performed this procedure many times. As the trial confirmed, most mothers feel their babies move more vigorously when, or soon after, the warmth is applied. Apart from adding to the safety and comfort of labour, this procedure emphasises the remarkable sensitivity of the unborn, and prematurely born, child — and the very special bond, the oneness, that exists between mother and child.

Extra-sensory perception

> Man has no Body distinct from his Soul; for that called Body is a portion
> of Soul discerned by the five Senses, the chief inlets of Soul in this age.
>   — WILLIAM BLAKE

Can we be influenced by 'extra-sensory' messages that otherwise explain common intuitive feelings? There is some experimental evidence emerging that our bodies have an extra-sensory awareness of being 'stared at'. The studies are designed to eliminate any chance of our other senses contributing to this awareness. One such study was performed in the late 1980s by Dr William Braud and colleagues at the Mind Science Foundation in San Antonio, Texas.[27] Subjects sat in an isolated room for 20 minutes in a relaxed state in front of a video camera.

An observer sat watching a monitor in another room, staring at the live image of the subjects at 30-second trial intervals. There were rest periods in between. The subject was connected to a device similar to a 'lie detector'; an electrode on the left hand recorded skin resistance, a measurement of the autonomic nervous system. The subject had no clues or guides indicating whether he or she was being stared at. The experiment was repeated with different subjects and observers. Significant differences in skin resistance were recorded at the times of the staring despite the subjects not being 'conscious' of it.

Research continues into whether 'distant healing' — prayer and intent — can have similar recordable effects on our bodies. Although responses do occur, the reasons for this have to be scrutinised. Factors such as hope, expectation and relaxation have to be accounted for before we have clearer hard evidence.[28]

This work examining these 'extra-sensory' areas is still in its infancy. Labels such as 'paranormal', 'psi' and 'parapsychology' have led to prejudice against these advances within the more conservative scientific community. But the quality of research into the so-called anomalous areas of prayer, human/machine interactions and extra-sensory perception is leading to a broadening of this view.

Whereas modern science is just beginning to take a close look at emotions and the 'subconscious' mind, traditional cultures have always linked the mind and the body together. For example, in Chinese medicine, the eye is known as the 'window of the soul'. The eye is not regarded simply as a receiver of visual information but also as a projector of emotion. The evolutionary biologist Rupert Sheldrake describes how snakes immobilise their prey through their gaze. This is the original meaning of the word 'fascination'. He goes on to observe that the word 'envy' is derived from the Latin *invidere*, to see intensively. In India, holy men and women are visited for their *darshan*, their look of love and compassion.[29]

I had the great fortune to meet a Tibetan lama several years back. As he looked at me, I felt his gaze enter through my eyes and go down somewhere deep into my chest. It was a most pleasant experience, a lovely gift from this humble, smiling monk.

I was reminded of this recently when watching a television documentary on the life of Adolf Hitler. An elderly man was recalling a meeting with Hitler at his holiday residence at Berchtesgaden. He described how Hitler transfixed him with a 'hypnotic' stare that penetrated him and seemed to go right into him. However, unlike my own experience, he was left feeling distinctly uneasy.

These stories are of course anecdotal but very powerful to those individuals who experience them. In Western medicine and culture these experiences contribute to the vast body of knowledge referred to as 'empirical'. The causes and reasons are, as yet, scientifically *unproven*. Unfortunately, this term is often misrepresented in the media as being synonymous with *disproven*. Mainstream science is slowly beginning to investigate these time-honoured observations. As they relate so closely to natural healing, it is unfair on those already suffering with chronic illnesses to wait decades for the scientific community to 'catch up'. *Empirical data* must be assessed and valued in its own right.

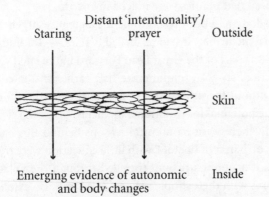

8. Chinese medicine

A working model of healing

To become more informed about healing, we must consider other models of health that have withstood the test of time. Models based on centuries of empirical evidence and meticulous recording. Models that are as free as possible from being tarnished by commercial self-interest or political gain. I will use Chinese medicine as an example of this as it has been an area of intense interest to me over the years.

When I started to study Chinese medicine in the early 1980s, I was in two minds about it. On the one hand I was excited because it seemed to provide a valid and logical reason why acupuncture worked. It also linked physical diseases holistically with emotions and environmental conditions, which made sense to me. However, it was taught as dogma with poorly constructed 'scientific' trials always claiming a 98 percent success rate. This part didn't ring true to me. Was I doing it wrong? Very soon I realised that politics were indeed involved.

Mao Ze-dong had been responsible for a great resurgence in the use of traditional medicine. He had relabelled it TCM — Traditional Chinese Medicine — as part of the Great Leap Forward in the late 1950s.[30] Traditional practices such as acupuncture had earlier in the century been practised without the official seal of approval from the ruling regimes. Mao saw the potential for traditional medicine.

Primarily, there were economical reasons behind this endorsement. Thousands of 'barefoot doctors' with little education were trained in the basic skills of acupuncture, and travelled through the villages treating many diseases with their simple recipes. TCM was also extolled as being unique to the Great Proletarian Cultural Revolution — an ideal propaganda tool.

In 1971, *New York Times* journalist James Reston suffered acute appendicitis while waiting to interview the Chinese leadership in Beijing. He duly underwent an emergency appendectomy but received acupuncture for his post-operative pain.[31] Intense interest turned on acupuncture and Chinese medicine. It was then heralded as the answer to many Western ills. It could cure obesity and stop us smoking. You could even use it instead of an anaesthetic!

If anything, these claims, and the promotion of TCM, have clouded and distorted the true value of Chinese medicine in the West. Too often Chinese medicine is dismissed because of these recent connections. We have to look beyond this, taking into account 2000 years of well-recorded 'empirical' data. My own interest was fuelled when I learned the bodymind links taught in Chinese medicine.

Chinese medicine accepts that changes in the weather and different emotional states affect the body. It also describes how and where they have an effect. Organ systems are seen to be affected to different degrees by these influences. The Chinese take their points of reference from nature itself. They apply the laws of nature they observe every day in the outside world to the internal workings of the body. The macrocosm reflected in the microcosm.

The Five Phases

The Laws of the Five Phases, or Five Elements, can be a source of confusion to the Western mind. However, it is both logical and understandable when one considers the holistic approach of the Chinese. They had neither the inclination nor the means — such as microscopes — to investigate the complex structural workings of the body. Their surgery was, in earlier times, primitive with such practices as dissection and autopsy performed rarely for cultural reasons. Their terms of reference were, therefore, from the world outside and the cosmos. Those used in Western medicine have primarily been reductionist from advances in biochemical research.

Chinese physicians and philosophers closely observed life around them. The elements were the components of the earth — wood and plants, fire, ash and earth, metals and minerals, and water. They all related to each other, nurturing and feeding off each other. For example, wood fed the fire that produced the ash that formed the earth and then the minerals that in turn attracted water through condensation, and the water fed the plants.

All naturally occurring cycles such as the seasons and our own life cycles were seen to fit into this life-enhancing pattern. (See figures a and b below.) The phases also relate to each other in a controlling fashion (figure c).

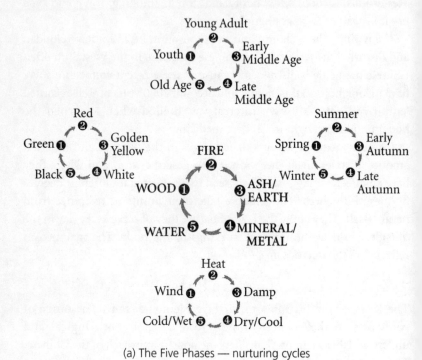

(a) The Five Phases — nurturing cycles

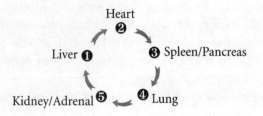

(b) The nurturing cycle — the vital organs

Wood *controls* Earth (retaining walls, roots hold up banks)

Earth *controls* Water (irrigation)

Water *controls* Fire

Fire *controls* Metals/minerals (forging steel, melting glass)

Metal *controls* Wood (axe to firewood)

(c) The controlling cycle

Visualisation:

Close your eyes and imagine yourself on a tropical island, resting under a gently swaying palm-tree (wood), feeling the warm sun (fire) on your face. You are lying on the soft sand (earth), listening to the gentle waves (water) as they break onto the golden beach. And the metal? In your hand is a can of your favourite cold drink, its surface glistening with condensation! All elements in perfect harmony.

Exercise

1. Study the three figures.
2. How many of these relationships ring true? Write them down — e.g., the autumn of my life, the restlessness of youth and the wind, the gold-yellow of a maturing harvest, etc.
3. Look at the nurturing and controlling elements. How do they relate to your experiences of life, nature and relationships?
4. Note how the vital organs of the body relate to each other, both in the nurturing and controlling cycles (Figures (b) and (c)). Note also their positions in the cycles, and how they 'correspond' with the other cycles.

Western mindbody medicine and Chinese medicine

So far, I have introduced you to evidence that *connections* inside and outside the body are vital to healing. Let's summarise this information before extending it in the way Chinese physicians see it:

◆ We are discovering communication networks between parts of the body we have been led to believe work in isolation.
◆ Our social networking, the diversity and quality of our relationships with other people, play a vital role in our healing.
◆ The prevailing mechanistic model of the body sees it as self-contained and isolated from these influences. However, even research within the restraints of this paradigm now recognises that we relate to the outside, through both our *autonomic* and *immune* systems.
◆ The effect on our body of extra-sensory forces, such as electro-magnetic fields, can also be measured scientifically. One such device, the SQUID* helmet, even records real-time images of our thought processes by measuring small variations in magnetic fields within our brains.[32]

In many ways, the Chinese have taken our 'evolving' healing model several steps further.

◆ They not only acknowledge that outside forces affect the body, they identify them and categorise the particular way this happens — i.e., how and why we feel irritable on a windy day.
◆ They do not separate the mind and the body. They take our new mindbody model one step further. Just as Candace Pert has identified clusters of peptide chemicals in various parts of the body that play a part in relaying our emotions, the Chinese describe emotional fields that relate to the vital — or *zang* — organs. The vital organs they describe are the heart, the spleen/pancreas, the lungs, the kidneys and the liver.
◆ They also describe how these relate to each other (see figures (a) and (b), page 114). The vital organs' importance is as much to do with the relationships between each other as with their own intrinsic

---

* Superconducting Quantum Interference Device.

workings. The body is far more than the sum of its parts. The connections and the balance add a vital dimension to our 'vitality', just as a group of people can work together in an effective team. They can both bring out the best in each other, while supporting each other in their weaker areas. However, it only takes one inconsiderate rogue to upset the others in the group.

◆ Chinese medicine, it must be remembered, had continued on a non-reductionist path. Only in recent years has China followed the prevailing Western model of health based on the Cartesian theory of the separation of the mind, the emotions and the spiritual from the 'mechanical' body.

The Chinese bodymind — the zang-fu

I first gained a deeper understanding of the *zang-fu*, the bodymind connections of the vital organs, in the late 1980s. A group of New Zealand doctors, who had been using acupuncture in their general practices for several years, invited a world authority on the *zang-fu* to run workshops in New Zealand.

This was Dr Anita Cignolini from Milan, Italy. As she described these links, I felt a sense of excitement. For years I had listened to patients give their accounts of their illnesses; they had been keen to let me know how they felt, and quite naturally usually expressed this in emotional rather than medical terms. How the different seasons affected their rheumatism. How they had taken up smoking again when they were sad. I started to jot down the names of patients alongside Dr Cignolini's descriptions of these relationships. Already more was making sense. But enlightening as it was, it felt more akin to a confirmation — merely repeating information already handed to me by many people who had consulted me.

At that time, however, there was no obvious scientific model that complied with these theories. It seemed clear that we were dealing with a different dimension to the body. Fields, energy, physics. I began to ask myself, and others, why these had been excluded from my medical training.

I decided to start to inform my patients of this new level of understanding. I found that most were intrigued, and indeed relieved, to have many of their own feelings validated. That a draught on the neck may have something to do with their Bell's palsy; why it feels better to have a good cry; why a hug works wonders.

However, my orthodox colleagues who had no experience of acupuncture could not be expected to react so warmly.

'No evidence of such connections,' remarked one.

'What's all this nonsense of the liver wind, and the heart fire?' another would say.

I had to be careful who I talked to. The doctors who had attended the course formed a tight and friendly group.

The zang-fu

The Chinese applied their Law of the Five Elements to the working relationships of the body's vital organs — the zang organs. These are the parts of our body that you can't remove or, if you do, they have to be replaced: the liver, heart, spleen/pancreas (see page 126), lungs and kidneys.

The fu organs are the hollow tube-like structures, less vital to our bodies: the gall-bladder, stomach, small and large intestine, and urinary bladder. In general, these organs can be removed either partly (e.g., the intestines and stomach) or wholly (e.g., the gall-bladder) without endangering our lives.

Organ	Western equivalent	Emotion	Climate
Liver	Liver, muscles, tendons	Creativity/anger	Wind/spring
Heart	Heart	Joy/mania	Hot/summer
Spleen	Immune system, pancreas, gut	Compassion/pity	Damp/late summer
Lung	Lung, respiratory tract, skin	Righteousness/grief	Dry/autumn
Kidney	Kidney, adrenals, bones	Sensitivity/fear	Cold/winter

The zang-fu correspondences

For those of us trained in the biological sciences, such correlations are difficult. These are organs we have studied in our anatomy books and even dissected in our anatomy rooms. They appear outlined on ultrasound scans, and in great detail on MRI and CT scans. No wonder giving these organs *feelings* seems strange. To many practitioners 15 years ago it was incomprehensible.

The separation of the mind and body dates back to the philosophies of Isaac Newton and René Descartes in the seventeenth century. It was deemed sensible then to leave matters of the soul to the Church. This released medical science from these controversial issues, allowing it to proceed with its study of the anatomy and chemistry of the body unimpeded.

Yet Western literature had never abandoned these mindbody connections. As Oscar Wilde somewhat despairingly remarked, 'Those who see any difference between soul and body have neither.'

The Romantic poets of the eighteenth and nineteenth centuries rallied against this mindset. The works of Blake, Wordsworth, Byron and Arnold are full of metaphysical images. There are many vivid examples within their poems of the very mindbody links described in the ancient Chinese texts. Here Matthew Arnold could well be quoting the words of a wise Chinese physician:

> We cannot kindle when we will
> The fire which in the heart resides
> The spirit bloweth and is still
> In mystery our soul abides.

Like Oscar Wilde years later, the Romantic poets were frustrated by the narrow-minded, fixed opinions of their times. In 1802 William Blake pleaded: '. . . may God us keep, from single vision, and Newton's sleep!'

These literal associations have survived to this day; we still use them in our daily language. 'His heart isn't in it.' 'He vented his spleen.' 'That took some guts' and 'I feel very liverish today'. It is interesting to compare how closely these links resemble the Chinese *zang-fu* associations observed independently on the other side of the world.

The Chinese believed that their form or structure was dependent on underlying energy fields, that they were primarily spiritual, energetic beings with physical form. This life energy was *qi*. So the physical presence of an organ such as the heart was only one aspect of a wider, more holistic phenomenon.

Modern science is only now studying the properties of energy and information fields — how one part of the body relates to another. For example, the magnetic fields of different parts of the brain are seen to overlap with a greater 'sharing of duties' than we once thought. The boundaries are more blurred than we imagined when studying the anatomy alone. Also the clustering of peptides, our molecules of emotion, at different bodily sites is drawing researchers towards studying these fields of influence. Our physical structure, e.g., how tall we grow and the colour of our eyes, is largely dictated by the DNA of our chromosomes. We inherit all the correct pieces of the jigsaw. But when we are a tiny foetus in the womb, what guides our pieces in the right direction and makes sure they fit? Where is our guide map?

We now know that we replace all our liver cells in six weeks. How do our cells know where to re-form? How come we replace diseased cells with more diseased cells? If we harbour deep grudges, and repress our anger and our grief, how come these emotions can be stuck for years inside us, even though all the cells in our organs have died off and been replaced?

These questions remain unanswered and are outside current scientific understanding. However, scientists with a broader vision are continuing to expand the boundaries of our knowledge by attempting to answer such questions. Meanwhile, we may consider some of the time-honoured observations of the Chinese enlightening.

The Chinese livermind

The liver is associated with the wood element. It represents new growth, youth and creativity. It represents the energy needed to get a project underway — brainstorming, entrepreneurship. It represents strength and direction. We are often motivated to start a new project because of frustration. We are spurred into action when we feel 'our hackles rise'. We write that letter to the papers when a politician offends us. Anger is used as a 'springboard' for action. We become animated and creative.

However, anger poorly channelled can be destructive. If our liver energy is not dealt with or soothed appropriately, it can explode outwardly in violence to others either with our tongues or our fists. Alternatively, it can work inwards, as resentment or angst, with destructive effects on our own body.

Alcohol can be seen to enhance the beneficial liver effects initially. We can become more expressive and less self-conscious after a couple of drinks. Many people become more creative at this point. But the danger is that too much alcohol brings out the destructive side of an imbalanced liver. Fuel to the fire. Aggressive, loud mouthed, abusive. Poor judgement. Close relationships suffer; a wider circle of friends and relatives are affected and suffer in some way.

Each *zang* organ has an associated sense organ. The liver is expressed in the eyes. The wide-eyed youth. Compare this with the angry red eyes of someone violent and drunk.

The liver is also the 'wind'. A free flow of ideas. The winds of change. When did you last 'fly off the handle'? The Chinese describe the liver as promoting the free flow of energy around the body. When it functions poorly we become 'uptight'. Our muscles become tense, we get headaches and stomach cramps. These symptoms may move confusingly around the body 'like the wind'.

An environment of wood, and the colour green, can soothe and harmonise the liver. A walk in the bush or even a game of golf is a great antidote to stress. It may have occurred to you that many of these 'liver' traits are particularly prominent in males. You may have also observed the oak-panelled walls so common in men's clubs, and in traditional male-only domains such as billiard halls.

The Chinese also treat raised blood pressure with herbs and acupuncture points known to harmonise the liver *qi*. But how much is hypertension due to tension? The most famous study in the West is the Framingham Heart Study, which has studied a whole community for risk factors for heart disease. Over 1000 men and women with normal blood pressures underwent physical and psychological tests before being followed up for 20 years. They found that 'among middle-aged men (45–59), but not women, anxiety levels were predictive of later incidence of hypertension.'[33]

Chinese medicine describes how pent-up frustrations may lead to other organs being damaged. It talks about the 'liver invading the spleen or stomach'. The modern equivalent of this occurs when an office worker such as Terry suffers from a duodenal ulcer.

Terry's story

Terry was trapped in middle management. At 55, he had 30 years of loyal service in the accounts department. In retrospect, he wished he'd gone to university; so many had been promoted to positions above him after fewer years in the firm. Two had even become directors less than 10 years after graduating.

Feeling despondent he had become tired and irritable, needing two or three Scotches at night to relax. Terry had also suffered indigestion for years, and carried with him a supply of chewable antacid tablets. His stomach pains were worsening and the tablets were having little effect. His doctor arranged for him to have an endoscopy, to view the lining of the stomach. There were signs of a duodenal ulcer, requiring more effective medication.

This story has a happy ending. Terry and his wife Ann talked about the situation. She was a trained nurse who had spent the past five years running a geriatric nursing home. Their two children had left home.

Terry sought redundancy and with the proceeds from this and the sale of their freehold home, they bought a guest house on the coast.

They now say they have never felt so satisfied with their lives. Terry's diligence and attention to detail and Ann's compassion and hard work have created a wonderfully relaxing holiday environment. Terry has stopped all his pills, and feels better than he has in years. Among their many visitors are his old work colleagues keen for a break away from their daily pressures.

'You got out at the right time,' they say.

The Chinese would say the root of Terry's problem was in the liver. But if we did simple blood tests, an ultrasound or a tissue biopsy, there would be no sign of a diseased liver. The Eastern and Western physicians would be in conflict, each one thinking the other a 'bit of an idiot'. I often act as an 'interpreter' in such disputes.

Better still, Terry should be fully informed of both ways of thinking with emphasis on where there is agreement. Terry would have much to gain from a deep understanding of the Chinese liver. When explained, many aspects of someone's life can fall into place, allowing him or her to make informed, healthy decisions. Just knowing this ancient wisdom is healing.

∽

The Chinese heartmind

Recently, a young woman came to see me having just started anti-depressant medication. All joy and fun had disappeared from her life. When she looked around, all she could see was a grey dreariness. The colour had gone. She lacked vitality; her eyes no longer sparkled.

Pointing to the middle of her chest, she told me: 'My heart is full of cold, heavy stones.'

The Chinese heart is the heart we talk about outside the hospital grounds. The heart that holds passion, that can be won or lost. Our heart's either in it, or it isn't. We can be light-hearted or, like this woman, heavy-hearted. Joyful or joyless.

When our heart energy is strong, we are 'running hot'. The Chinese heart is the fire element — high summer, when the colours are at their brightest.

We fall in love and give our hearts to someone. When we hug, we join hearts. The Chinese meridians associated with heart run down the arm into the palms. When we hold hands we join hearts. When we shake hands, we do the same rather more formally. We clap our hands to applaud a performer who has sung from the heart.

The tip of the tongue is also an area associated with the heart in Chinese medicine. Chinese physicians will study this area closely, especially if the eyes are not sparkling — no *shen* — and the pulse is weak. Tongues join in more passionate embraces.

If the heart energy is too exaggerated, we can become euphoric, even manic — the other pole of bipolar depressive illness. We do not feel the need to sleep. We rush around spending money, accruing huge phone bills, gambling our life savings away. Spike Milligan, the comedian and author, has done much to bring this condition to the public's attention.[34] A lifetime sufferer of bipolar illness, he explains that many of his best *Goon Show* scripts were created when he was sick. These are thought by many to be works of genius. We now have the expertise to isolate the gene that is responsible for bipolar disorder — previously known as manic-depression. This also means we could identify carriers of this gene pre-natally with the choice of aborting the foetus.

Kay Redfield Jamieson, a professor of psychiatry at Johns Hopkins School of Medicine, Maryland, raises the ethical and moral concerns that surround this issue. If this technology had been readily available centuries ago, she suggests the world may have had no Vincent van Gogh, no Paul Gauguin, no Gustav Mahler or Lord Byron, no Samuel Taylor Coleridge, Ernest Hemingway or Virginia Woolf.[35]

We have already mentioned some areas where Western and Eastern medical ideas clash. None more so than over the Chinese notion of the heart. I frequently see patients who have seen TCM practitioners who have taken their pulses and told them they have weak hearts. In the West, we fear heart disease; it makes us feel very mortal. On several occasions, despite explaining the different paradigms, patients have needed full investigations — ECGs, cardiac ultrasound — to be reassured they weren't about to have a heart attack. However, it is becoming increasingly clear that emotions play a major role in heart and circulatory disorders.

One 1996 study of 268 men and 35 women with known coronary artery disease investigated the role of personality in long-term mortality. It found that over a quarter (27 percent) of the patients with a type-D personality — a tendency to suppress emotional distress — died within 10 years compared with only 7 percent of the 'controls'. The groups were balanced with regard to the well-known biomedical risk factors of smoking, cholesterol and age.[36]

Another study in 1994 on 119 middle-aged men in Finland investigated the effect of hostility and anger suppression on their diseased carotid arteries (the large arteries in the neck). The researchers studied the arteries with ultrasound, and used psychological questionnaires to measure traits related to anger and distrust. When all the other variables were balanced out, they found that the disease progressed twice as quickly in the group with 'high cynical distrust and high anger control'.[37] Other recent trials have shown that men with heart disease are at increased risk if:

◆ They reported few persons to whom they gave or received social support.[38]
◆ They had a small number of friends.[38]
◆ They were not married.[38]
◆ They were not members of clubs or groups.[38, 39]
◆ They lacked religious 'strength and comfort'.[39]

One large review in 1993, in the journal *Psychosomatics*,[40] studied over 50 papers, concluding that: 'Anger, depression and anxiety play a major role in the genesis of ischaemic heart disease'.

The review's author, M. W. Ketterer, also makes the following comment:

> Resistance to the utility of this avenue of care is not based on evidence alone, because widely accepted risk factors and/or treatment modalities often have less persuasive evidence, or less powerful effects, than do emotional factors. Rather such resistance is largely due to *paradigmatic scotomata* — conceptual difficulties for those not familiar with biopsychosocial research.

Here he is pleading for a broader vision than one dictated to by the reductionist paradigm associated with Isaac Newton and René Descartes. *Scotomata* are blind spots. Nearly two centuries later, he is voicing the very concerns of William Blake, in more comprehensive but rather less poetic terms.

Fortunately, this research is being heeded by some. The landmark 'Lifestyle Heart Trial' by Dr Dean Ornish and associates in 1990 provided evidence that coronary artery disease could actually regress with intense lifestyle changes.[41] These included more extreme dietary measures — vegetarianism rather than just an adherence to a low-fat diet — and the use of stress management techniques such as meditation, breathing and imagery. The width of the heart vessels were measured before and a year after patients made such changes. The results were remarkable.

Of those in the group who made these changes, 82 percent had a reduction in the narrowing of their arteries, compared with 42 percent in the control group. Over half the control group had more narrowing, representing a progression of the disease. Lifestyle changes alone could potentially reverse coronary artery disease.

Over the past decade, this study has led to other trials with the focus on less invasive tests — scans rather than angiograms — and on longer-term outcomes. Dean Ornish's results are being confirmed although some studies show weaker benefits after two years of less stringent changes.[42, 43]

In China, acupuncture has been widely used for heart conditions such as angina pectoris. There they follow the traditional principles I have already outlined, using their version of the holistic mindbody approach. There have been a few encouraging trials in the West on the benefits of acupuncture in angina.[44, 45] But when it comes to integrating holistic medicine with conventional cardiology, I am conscious of trying to awaken a profession from a very deep *Newton's sleep*.

I have been fortunate, however, to have treated a number of angina sufferers referred by doctors after 'conventional methods' have resulted in poor control. My own experience suggests that this is an area where Eastern and Western physicians must join hands.

Most of us have heard Rudyard Kipling's famous line: 'Oh, East is East, and West is West, and never the twain shall meet.'

We frequently overlook that he goes on:

> But there is neither East nor West,
> Border, nor breed, nor birth,
> When two strong men stand face to face,
> Though they come from the ends of the earth!

The Chinese spleenmind

The spleen is a compact organ tucked under our left ribs, high in our abdomen. It makes and destroys blood cells. It eliminates invaders such as bacteria and produces antibodies. It is not as vital as the other organs but children, in particular, can be prone to serious infection from the bacterium pneumococcus if they are not immunised following the surgical removal of the spleen.

The Chinese 'spleen' is described by some writers as the spleen/pancreas. The nearby pancreas is definitely an essential organ, producing both insulin and pancreatic juices to aid digestion. The function of the Chinese spleen covers:

◆ Blood production and storage (spleen);
◆ Immunity and defence (spleen);
◆ Transporting and transforming energy around the body (pancreas — insulin allows glucose to be absorbed into our cells);
◆ Digestion and bowel function (pancreas).

As we have seen with the other vital organs, the Chinese spleen is a mindbody spleen. It is the organ of the earth element: and the humid, early autumn when golden-yellow crops are harvested, and fruit matures:

> Season of mists and mellow fruitfulness
> Close bosom friend of the maturing sun
> Conspiring with him how to load and bless
> With fruit the vines that round the thatch-eaves run.
>
> — KEATS, 'TO AUTUMN'

A balanced 'spleen' is compassionate, nurturing and giving but has a strong sense of self. When balance is lost, compassion for others can turn inwards. Brooding, worry and self-pity may result. Physically we may feel bogged down, heavy and sluggish. Just as the wind affects the liver, dampness affects the spleen.

And because the Chinese spleen stores the blood, weakness may result from bruising and heavy menstrual loss in women.

Before we investigated the spleen scientifically in the West, it also had strong links with the emotions. It was known as the 'seat of emotions'. When we 'vent our spleens', all our bottled-up rage escapes. The Chinese spleen probably sits closer to the other old English association with melancholy, feeling generally miserable and sorry for ourselves.

> To cure mind's wrong bias, Spleen,
> Some recommend the bowling green.
>
> — MATTHEW GREEN, 1696–1737

If the rather aggressive, impulsive liver is seen as a more masculine characteristic, then the nurturing stability of the spleen is far more feminine, the Earth Mother. Young men may sow their wild oats but women have to give birth, love and comfort their 'offspring'.

The Law of the Five Phases shows two ways the male energy can affect the female.

The first way is through part of the controlling cycle (see figure below). Just as Terry's liver energy 'attacked his stomach', so controlling aggressive male behaviour — violence, sexual assault — damages the very fabric of our society, the nurturing love and care of women. When the same controlling forces are used on the environment, Mother Earth, *Gaia*, is also seen to suffer. Acknowledging this has led to the birth of *eco-feminism* in the past few years. The debate on genetically engineered foods may also be seen in this light.

Women, in particular, are wary of the effects these unnatural controls may have on their own and their children's bodies. They are responding to their survival instincts. No amount of debate from rational but emotionally distant scientists will ever sway them.

The second way the liver and spleen can achieve an ideal balance is through the nurturing cycle.

This time it passes through the organ of love and passion, the heart (see figure below). Cupid strikes!

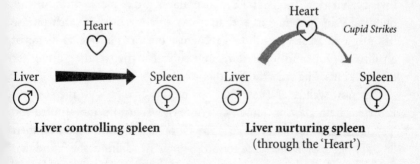

Liver controlling spleen **Liver nurturing spleen**
(through the 'Heart')

Already we can see a model which, in its own way, can explain the findings of our modern mindbody studies. The consistent references to the
value of close, quality relationships and of having a diverse group of
social contacts. Our lives are delicately balanced, and loving intent is
essential to healing.

We know how close relationships can enhance our health and
immunity. Strong evidence is emerging now to support the mindbody
picture of the 'spleen' painted by ancient Chinese physicians. Recent
studies have shown that psychological stress increases our susceptibility
to colds and respiratory infection. It has been shown that we actually
catch colds more easily when stressed; it is not merely that the symptoms
feel worse.[46]

Another study investigated 90 newlywed couples, submitting them to
psychological questioning of marital problems.[47] They were monitored
for 'problem-solving behaviour patterns', and blood samples were taken
to assess changes in the activity of the immune system. These included
how the natural killer cells performed, antibody levels, and the total
number of lymphocytes (white blood cells) present. Those subjects who
exhibited more 'negative or hostile' behaviour were shown to have the
more poorly performing immune systems. The women in the trial were
more affected than the men, establishing yet another bridge between
modern Western research and ancient Eastern wisdom.

How many times have you asked yourself, or your doctor, why you are
catching every bug around? Why does your husband or wife avoid the
misery of these infections if it is just a matter of breathing in these
invisible viruses? In general practice, never a day passes without this
question being posed. Rather than trot out that well-worn catch-phrase
'It's just a virus', doctors should recognise the virus as one co-factor of
an illness. Our emotional state, and probably the weather, are other
factors — just like our grandmothers told us.

It is now well established that our moods change with the seasons.
Professor Beth Dawson-Hughes of Tufts University, Boston, studied 250
'psychiatrically normal women' aged 43 to 72, and confirmed that their
levels of depression increased towards winter. In addition, she found that
there were marked increases in tension, hostility and 'feelings of bewilderment' during autumn.[48]

Other physical changes have also been noted. Women tend to put on more fat around their waists in winter, while losing bone mass in compensation.[49]

Although we are still a long way from proving all the subtle and intricate mind/body/weather relationships described in Chinese medicine, we are seeing Western thought opening up to these broader, more holistic principles.

In many ways, it shifts the balance of power away from the investigator with a microscope back to those whose lives are directly exposed to these infections. While in no way detracting from important public health measures such as immunisation protocols, professionals who ignore these issues run the risk of alienating an increasingly aware public. Women in particular must be allowed to be fully informed, as their bodies and those of their children seem particularly vulnerable to neglect and abuse.

❧

The Chinese lungmind

Our lungs are truly vital organs. We have to breathe all the time or else we die. Life begins for us as we take our first breath at birth. From that very moment we are connected to the outside world, breathing in essential oxygen atoms that enrich our blood and continually update us with vital information about the world around us. This oxygen is the gift from the world's plants; they breathe out oxygen as a waste product of photosynthesis. In this process, photons of light from the sun convert water and carbon dioxide into complex organic matter vital to the plant. So in two quick steps, we are instantly connected to our own world and the solar system.

So the Chinese lung energy is pure and special. It corresponds to the 'colour' white — pure as the driven snow. Traditionally brides have worn white in more innocent times to honour virginity. We tell white lies; the virtuous white knight battles the forbidding black knight.

The lungs act at the interface of this pure energy and the body. Breathing in draws it downwards into the body, where it mixes with our blood, lightening it. Dark purple venous blood becomes bright red arterial blood. The Chinese talk of the lung as the organ that joins the *corporeal* with the *ethereal* soul — the visible with the invisible.

They also link the lungs with the skin. Initially this may appear strange to our Western way of thinking. However, both the skin and our lungs are our organs of contact with the air — both arise from the same embryological tissue layer, the ectoderm. The link between asthma and the skin condition eczema is well known in Western medicine, and acupuncture points on the lung meridian are used for both these conditions.

Chinese use acupuncture and herbs to 'tonify the lung' when someone is susceptible to frequent respiratory infections, often treating the 'spleen' as well to enhance general immunity.

Smoking tobacco can also act as a lung tonic but it pollutes the purity of the breath. When someone stops smoking, their skin colour improves and their eyes sparkle again. This is some consolation for the grief of losing a trusted, but very conditional 'friend'. Often in the following weeks, the ex-smoker gets every cold going, frequently complaining bitterly about the unfairness of it all.

Grieving involves the lung. We wail, cry and sob at the loss of a loved one. In many cultures, it is common to see bereaved spouses beating their chests while 'lost in grief'. Singing, crying and gentle laughter are all seen as important healing ingredients at funerals and memorial services.

Before the discovery of antibiotics half a century ago, tuberculosis was treated primarily with rest and fresh air. In nineteenth century England large sanitaria were built on the warmer south coast to escape the damp, polluted air of the cities. Some had annexes made of glass, as in modern conservatories, shielding patients from the cold and damp. Others had open-air verandas large enough to hold beds. Some families even emigrated to Australia for the warmer dry air and the less crowded conditions.

Modern drugs, and improved social conditions have played a major part in reducing the incidence and severity of many lung diseases. However, the incidence of asthma, where the lining of the lung overreacts to allergens and invaders, is climbing at an alarming rate in the developing world. Either we are becoming more sensitive to our environment or our environment is becoming more toxic. Most likely is that both these conditions are true.

Western medicine, by and large, has ignored sensitivity as it has proved difficult to measure. Research funds have been siphoned into the development of sophisticated drugs — that when inhaled work to suppress overactive airways in asthmatic patients. This has been successful in reducing symptoms, and even deaths from asthma.

However, ancient wisdom provides many deep insights into the functions of the lung, which should redirect research into more holistic areas. With our modern Western 'diaphragmatic' breathing exercises, we are beginning to treat our lungs with the reverence shown by the teachers of yoga and *qi-gong*. As the Indian Sufi teacher Hazrat Inayat Khan described nearly a century ago:

> Breath is the very life of beings, and what holds all the particles of the body together is the power of the breath. As the power of the sun holds all the planets, so the power of the breath holds every organ.

~

The Chinese kidneymind

The House of Essence

'. . . think of that — a man of my kidney — think of that . . .'
— WILLIAM SHAKESPEARE, *THE MERRY WIVES OF WINDSOR*

The Chinese mindbody kidney has functions and characteristics that at first can seem confusing and esoteric. They see the 'kidney' in humans much as we see the roots of a plant. The deepest organ that houses our *essence*, and governs our *will*. In *The Merry Wives of Windsor* Falstaff was complaining bitterly of the way he had just been treated. In the sixteenth century a person's 'kidney' referred to his personality, resolve and temperament. In Chapter 2, Chloe dealt with cancer by affirming life, drawing on an inner *will to live*.

As Sir Walter Scott wrote:

> Forward and frolic glee was there
> The will to do, the soul to dare.

As many of the stories in this book show, it is willpower that so often pulls people through the most trying illnesses. It is truly an essential ingredient of deep healing, with the healer being constantly guided and enriched by this mysterious force. When working in partnership, the healer and patient perform as one, in perfect harmony. When agendas clash, as I was to find with Henrietta, a powerful battle can ensue.

Henrietta's story

My very first day of general practice brought me face to face with Henrietta. I had some prior warning. The practice nurse had at morning tea explained that Henrietta, a single lady in her late seventies, expected a monthly house call for her Vitamin B12 injection. She was confined to her bed, and had been so for some time.

I keenly perused her notes in search of a clue to her diagnosis — several frayed cards, with fading handwriting dating back 30 years. All I could discover was that Henrietta had taken to her bed in 1955 for reasons that for 26 years had remained obscure. She was looked after by her younger sister who prepared her meals and kept the house spotless. There were, apparently, frequent visitors to the house, mainly elderly friends who would sit by her bed listening to Henrietta's wise words of advice. I was to meet one some time later who referred to her as a 'saint'.

So in a state of some bewilderment, I headed off to her home to be met at the door by a rather tired elderly looking sister. Henrietta greeted me cordially, immediately presenting her arm for the vitamin shot. I duly obliged, before asking to examine her. I was informed that this wasn't necessary but somehow I managed to check her heart and blood pressure. I also noted no pressure sores. Beside her bed was a small jam jar, quarter full with brandy.

Like three doctors before me, I initially queried the worth of this monthly ritual. She always wanted me, not the practice nurse, and any attempt by me to reduce the frequency of these calls was unsuccessful.

After three years, her sister had a stroke and was admitted to a geriatric ward. Henrietta demanded a live-in nurse, but with no diagnosis I was unable to find one.

I was left with only one option — to admit Henrietta, against her will, to the local hospital. No mean task, as it meant recounting the whole tale to an overworked hospital doctor on a Friday evening. I gave her one final check-over. Henrietta glared at me throughout, complaining bitterly about being moved and chastising me for my inability to keep her at home.

The ambulance duly arrived and Henrietta was stretchered out of her house. I locked up, handing her the keys. I wished her well, but she looked away. At home two hours later, the phone rang. It was the admitting doctor sounding worried and confused.

'What was wrong with her?' he asked. He too had examined her and had found no abnormality. Henrietta wouldn't talk to him. He had then gone out of the admitting room to write out a form for a chest X-ray, part of the routine in those days. When he returned, Henrietta was dead.

As with the Chinese 'spleen', the kidney is a broad term that also covers the organs that sit directly above the anatomical structures, the adrenal glands. Included too are the sexual and the reproductive organs, which arise from the same embryological zone — the urogenital ridge.

So the functions of the Chinese kidney are profound. Some closely correspond to our scientific understanding of the kidney and adrenal glands:

1. Fear and sensitivity: In Western terms these relate to the basic survival instinct of fight, fright and flight. The adrenal hormones adrenalin and noradrenaline work alongside, and in response to, the sympathetic nervous system.
2. Fluid, mineral balance and blood pressure control: This complies with the Western model where the kidney filters out impurities in the blood, controlling the balance of fluid and vital minerals. Hormones from the kidney and adrenal glands are involved.
3. Bone growth, and maturation: The kidney is involved in the manufacture of Vitamin D which is vital for bone growth.
4. Immune balance and stress: Cortisol from the adrenal cortex modifies fat and glucose metabolism, immune function and the effects of adrenaline. It is known to be produced as a result of stress, through hormonal pathways from the brain. Its regulation is impaired by depression and ageing. The measurement of cortisol in the blood is now used as a chemical measurement of the amount of stress on the body.

So the Eastern holistic view of this region of the body closely corresponds to Western science. However, Eastern philosophies expand this model into areas such as *will*, so far excluded from reductionist science.

Traditional Chinese and Indian cultures stress the importance of drawing the energy of the macrocosm — the breath — deep within the body. In Chinese medicine this corresponds to the lower *jaio*, or that area which contains the kidney. In Ayurvedic medicine it corresponds to the lower *chakras*. The breath is 'received by the kidney', mixing the essence of the cosmos with the uniqueness of the person. In Chinese medicine the kidney *qi* then distributes this gently upwards to the other organs. Nothing is forced, with the individual's character and sensitivities honoured and fed.

The kidney corresponds naturally to the water element. Also to winter, decay and old age. But ageing and dying are seen as necessary parts of the life cycle. A vital process allowing birth and new growth.

Whereas the lung is 'white', the kidney is 'black'. The Chinese diagnose kidney deficiency by observing dark rings under the eyes. They also link the kidney to the sense of hearing. We have already discussed how music can reach profound emotional depths within us. John Milton gives us a vivid image of this power of hearing in 'Comus':

> I was all ear
> And took in strains that might create a soul
> Under the ribs of death

Classical disorders of the kidneys occur at times of great transition in someone's life. Chinese medicine sees many changes of the menopause as having their roots in the 'kidney' — sweats, palpitations, hot flushes, vaginal dryness. To these can be added many, less definable, feelings such as apprehension and phobias.

Menopause heralds a significant change in the life of a woman. A time when she can discover her true self, her true essence. A time when her sensitivity can be honoured creatively, away from the overwhelming demands of a wife and mother.

Our biochemical model does not yet allow for this broad, holistic view. Of all the Chinese mindbody organs, the kidney is the most difficult to explain in Western terms. It deals with our spiritual roots, our uniqueness. Maybe too, we are only beginning to understand the role of the largest component of the human body, water. Our water molecules far outnumber our body's protein molecules and yet we know very little about water's role in our bodies. There were no lectures on water when I was at medical school; it was viewed merely as the body's dilutant.

We shall explore how water can play its role as a holder of memory, and a transmitter of information in Chapter 10. We know that whales communicate with each other at great distances — hundreds of kilometres — by emitting low frequency sound. Water transmits these frequencies highly efficiently, and researchers are exploring the possibility that a similar mechanism underlies the transfer of information along acupuncture meridians. Fish are known to possess *lateral lines* along their bodies that receive both sound and touch vibrations. These allow them to sense the presence of their own species for 'polarised schooling', and also to detect prey. So survival, sensitivity, 'hearing' and water all form an association for underwater creatures which is not far removed from the Chinese concept of the human 'kidney'.

In the near future, understanding the physical nature of water may not only help explain such phenomena as acupuncture and homoeo-pathy, it may begin to tell us a great deal more about ourselves.

Using Nature

There is a pleasure in the pathless woods,
There is a rapture in the lonely shore,
There is society where none intrudes
By the deep sea, and music in its roar.
I love not man the less, but Nature more.
— LORD BYRON, *CHILDE HAROLD'S PILGRIMAGE*, IV. 178

The wise observations of the Chinese, which linked the interactions of nature with those of the body, can be put to good use. Travel brochures tempt us to holiday on tropical islands with their seductive blend of warm water, palm trees, and spectacular sunsets. But Eastern medicine and phi-losophy teaches us to become connoisseurs of the healing powers of nature. Rather than be satisfied with blends, we begin to identify specific antidotes to our problems. Many of these we have already discovered, as we respond to our instincts — relaxing in a warm bath after a hard day and a walk on a 'lonely shore' or in a 'pathless wood'.

Gravitating towards these environments is therapeutic in itself. Even without added effort, nature has a way of soothing even the most restless souls. But we can enhance the effects considerably if we open ourselves up to our surroundings using the exercises I described earlier in Chapter 3. The breath and meditation exercises move our bodies into a 'receiving mode'. And nature is generous with its gifts. It is so difficult for us to receive unconditionally from fellow humans. We may consider their needs, we may even feel guilty. With nature, it is less complicated.

Nevertheless, those indigenous cultures who still live in close contact with nature do so with great respect for their environment. Whenever healing rituals are performed by Native American Indians using the forces of nature, valued gifts such as tobacco are first offered, together with their heartfelt thanks.

This is a good example to follow as we learn to use the environment as an aid to healing. Be aware you are receiving a special gift, and acknowledge your gratitude in a way that is special to you.

Soothing the liver — plants and trees

In Chinese medicine the liver corresponds to the wood element. Liver imbalances frequently lead to symptoms of tension, irritability and restlessness. A shady wood provides calm and shelter with trees standing firm and stable. Even if there is wind rustling the tree's uppermost branches, its trunk and roots are firm. Green leaves and ferns are soothing to the eye. In Ayurvedic medicine, green balances the heart *chakra*. In Chinese medicine it harmonises the liver. Either way, green is soothing. The following exercises can be practised in a forest, wood, or even in your back garden. If you live in a city highrise apartment, sit on your balcony with a pot plant or bonsai tree (and your imagination).

Exercise

1. Breathing
Find a quiet spot by a tree where you can sit in some comfort. Leaning back against the tree is ideal.

Receive the breath into your abdomen as we have shown before. Allow all tension to drop from your shoulders. Relieve yourself of those responsibilities that weigh so heavily on you.

Close your eyes, and become aware of the subtle aromas of the surroundings as you breathe in.

Remember the inner smile.

2. Meditation
Allow your thoughts to come and go while focusing on your breath. Notice your whirling brain unwind.

Adapt your meditation practice to suit. Either focus on a leaf or fern or close your eyes, allowing your awareness to shift to the aromas or gentle rustling of leaves.*

---

* Dr Steven Aung, my friend and teacher from Alberta, Canada, strongly advises caution if the forest is known to be inhabited by grizzly bears! In this situation, he finds a deep state of relaxation is rarely achieved.

Touching trees can also be of great benefit. Many disparaging comments are made about tree huggers, often from people who are embarrassed to try this. But it is truly one of life's simple pleasures. The world is full of secret tree huggers. The next time you are in a furniture showroom, watch how many people stroke, caress and fondle the surface of the tables and dressers. Next time you are in a pub, watch the guy with the pool cue, and the guy leaning against the bar.

Bruce Lee, the martial arts legend, practised exercises receiving energy from trees. The secret to combative martial arts is the ability to harness one's strength without losing one's temper and control in combat. The Eastern traditions see trees, with their noble presence, strength and 'liver-soothing' properties as ideal role models and training aids for martial arts.

Getting it off your chest — the Lion's Roar

Tension and frustration often build up inside us, unable to be easily released. This is one reason we love to yell at football matches, often venting our bottled-up anger onto the hapless match referee. We safely assume he'll neither hear nor identify us, and being unable to leave the field could do little to retaliate anyway.

Road rage provides a similar outlet for modern day frustration. This time the car, not the crowd, provides our safety blanket, our armour. The seemingly quiet, mild-mannered Mr Hydes who walk on the pavements seem to turn into noisy, aggressive Dr Jeckylls behind the wheel. It wouldn't be too bad if it stopped there. But as we know, this behaviour is spilling out from our sports stadiums and our cars onto the streets with dire consequences.

The Lion's Roar is for all those who feel themselves slipping into these bad habits.

Exercises

1. The Set Up
The ideal environment for the Lion's Roar is where there is natural movement, wind and background noise — a wild, windswept beach, for example, with the sound of breakers crashing onto the shore. Alternatively, it could be a large waterfall. Imagine that the wind, water and waves are there to carry away your discarded frustrations.

If you are stuck in the city, confined to your highrise city apartment, try standing out on your deck on a windy day. Let the wind, and the traffic below you, drive your problems away.

2. The Lion's Roar

Stand with your back to the wind, feet slightly apart, hands together resting on each other over the middle of your abdomen (see figure a).

Breathe in slowly and deeply, while you raise your hands up towards your chest (see figure b).

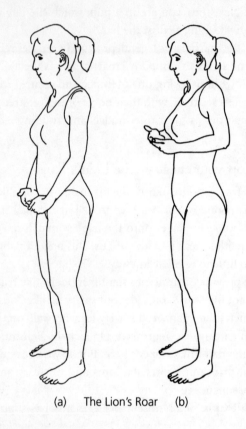

(a)   The Lion's Roar   (b)

After a brief pause, breathe out with some force and at the same time emit a Lion's Roar. Gesture with your hands, 'pushing' the roar away from your chest (see figure on facing page).

NB. Do not overstrain your voice. If you feel hoarse, do not repeat the exercise the same day.

You may find practising the Lion's Roar in company rather embarrassing — even within the apparent safety of a group. I felt intimidated when I first tried this. We attracted quite a crowd of bemused tourists while we learned this technique on the viewing platform overlooking the Huka

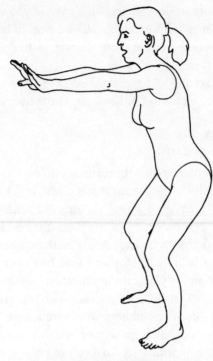

(c) The Lion's Roar

Falls near Taupo, New Zealand. Once you become bolder, I have found it wise to warn friends and family of this practice, especially if you are prone to acts of spontaneity!

Now I always warn patients in my waiting room before I demonstrate this exercise in my office. I have found that new patients, especially those who have come for their first acupuncture treatment, become concerned on hearing the roars coming from the treatment room. They tend to head towards the carpark, making last-minute excuses such as 'You know what, doc, my problem's just gone. It's a miracle'. No amount of reassurance after the event seems to be effective.

Heart-warming

The heart in Chinese medicine corresponds to the fire element. We talk of the warm and cold hearted. The words 'heart' and 'hearth' have similar old English roots. We are drawn to an open fire whether inside or out. A great place to gather around. Hugging is a great way to warm someone's heart. A mother applying a mentholated ointment to her child instinctively rubs this over the centre chest. It's where children — and some adults — cuddle their teddies.

So the heart exercise is simple. Either cuddle up to a loved one next to the fire, or rest a wheat bag or hot water bottle over your breast plate (sternum).

Getting down to earth

Tending to your garden, feeling the earth in your hands, watching it give sustenance to new life — these simple acts give so much satisfaction and pleasure. Many sufferers of severe rheumatoid arthritis, even when moving their hands provokes agonising pain, still tend lovingly to their gardens. A woman's deep understanding of the cyclical nature of life gives her a natural affinity to Mother Earth. In return, it can give her great comfort at times of physical, emotional and spiritual pain.

Recently in New Zealand, a media campaign was launched encouraging people to 'dob-in' neighbours who were known to be receiving disability benefits, and who were seen to be active around their homes and gardens. One lady with severe arthritis came to me in tears, afraid to venture out into her garden for fear of being reported. Sometimes our society seems to get it so wrong.

The next time you are gardening, be mindful of its therapeutic qualities. Wallow in the texture of the soil. Scoop out some of the earth with your fingers, and pat down the earth around a plant with your hands. Close your eyes while you do this.

When we are at home, we are also 'earthed'. We are now a highly mobile society; it's not only our jobs and schooling that force us to uproot. We move 'up' to better neighbourhoods, longing for security and capital gain. I see many people living in beautiful houses but still 'homeless'. Houses are 'done up' to be sold for a profit whereupon the cycle is repeated. Somewhere along the way, the fundamental need for a home is ignored. The unsettled body may indicate this need in many ways — insomnia, anxiety attacks, depression — especially in women caught in this trap.

Animals often form special bonds with their homes. Dogs may find their way back home despite being lost hundreds, even thousands, of kilometres away. Homing pigeons find their lofts even if these are moved while they are away. Even the simple shellfish, the limpet, has a remarkable homing ability![50] Biologist Rupert Sheldrake has reviewed all the literature on this fascinating subject.[29] Many of the previously widely held beliefs — i.e., that animals track their way home using the earth's magnetic field or through celestial navigation — fail to withstand scientific scrutiny. He suggests that these animals form special bonds with their homes that allow them to find their homes even when the homes move. Although we as yet have no scientific proof of this, most of us who move homes are surprised by the degree of stress and grief it causes. For many older people, as Henrietta dramatically demonstrated, moving can lead to a deterioration of health or even death.

Air and water

'Water, air and cleanness are the chief articles in my pharmacy.'
— NAPOLEON BONAPARTE

We have already talked extensively about savouring the air we breathe. Just as tuberculosis sufferers traditionally sought cures in the country and sea air, over time many have sought relief from their everyday stresses by retreating to spa towns.

Water has always held a special role in hygiene and healing. As a boy, I watched with fascination each time a trusted officer from the St John Ambulance Brigade rushed on to the rugby field with great urgency to aid an injured player, armed solely with a bucket of water and an orange sponge.

Every injury, at every anatomical site, received the same treatment protocol. This, as far as I could detect, involved thoroughly saturating the sponge with water before wiping the injured part with some considerable force. The officer would then wring out his sponge, rushing off the field, invariably managing to spill most of the contents of the bucket in the process.

If the injured man showed signs of concussion, the sponge was wrung out with great enthusiasm over the befuddled player's head. He would then be assisted to his feet to the appreciative cheers of the crowd. If he didn't immediately fall over, the procedure was judged a complete success. The player would then stagger back to the scene of conflict, while our hero ran confidently from the pitch, a proud and fulfilled man.

Modern, and safe, scientific sports medicine has now replaced this entertaining ritual; caution over blood-borne infections such as hepatitis and HIV viruses means bloodied players are exiled to the 'blood bin'; the concussed are scanned and 'stood down' for a month.

Water revitalises. A cold shower or a plunge into cool water makes us feel alive. Sure, we may curse, only to gloat at those who have yet to jump that 'it's really warm when you get used to it'. But despite the yelling and screaming, notice how everyone manages to smile and laugh through their shivering. A surf beach is a great place to shed tension — stresses are literally washed away.

Stiller, warmer waters are for wallowing — mindful swimming. The next time you are in a quiet pool or in some placid waters, try closing your eyes. While gently swimming breast stroke, feel the water lapping evenly against your skin. Try to continue to focus solely on this silky sensation with each stroke you make, and as soon as your mind wanders, re-focus back to this tactile sensation.

Similarly, rain can be wonderfully therapeutic. So the next time it is raining, get out and enjoy it. If it is warm, wear as little as you can get away with. Try closing your eyes, holding out your arms and whirling around, revelling in your rain massage. On the other hand, if it is cold, wrap up well and stand outside under a large umbrella. Focus on the sound of the rain on the umbrella. Take no notice of your neighbours.

And if the storm is electricial, stay inside and watch Gene Kelly in *Singing in the Rain*.

9. Healing patterns

Healing — from the inside, out

Have you ever wondered why that sore throat starts the moment you get home on a Friday evening? Why that migraine ruins the weekend, disappearing magically on Sunday night? Why you always get a cold on the second day of your holiday?

Sometimes our bodies appear particularly cruel, preventing us from doing the very things we enjoy. Are they just talking to us when they think we're listening? Is there any logic to this process?

These are some of the despairing questions that continue to be asked at my office every day. The best explanation I have found is in Chinese medicine and its explanation of the *Six Energetic Layers*. Before we explore this concept, we should examine how the body heals after being invaded by a visible object such as a splinter.

If the splinter is not removed quickly, an inflammatory reaction occurs. Pus then forms into an abscess as the body attempts to expel the invader through its surface, back to the outside world where it belongs. Tracts can form from the body to any surface that 'meets' the outside world — i.e., the bowel, bladder and genital tract in the form of *fistulae*. Bullets can track themselves out of the body, often emerging at the skin years after the initial injury.

Open wounds heal by granulation from the 'base up'.

If we eat something disagreeable, we vomit it out. Our bowels 'hurry' unwanted matter out, in the form of diarrhoea. If we breathe in dust, pollen, viruses or smoke, our noses run and our bronchial tubes contract and secrete mucus, making us expel these invaders by coughing.

143

We release tension out of the body by crying tears.

We tend to view all these 'bodily acts' as annoying symptoms, especially when they are spoiling our fun. Sometimes, with asthma or a post-operative fistula, medical attention is needed to prevent serious complications. But the basis of all these patterns is the attempt of the body to heal.

The concept of the Energetic Layers sees this pattern extended to cover deeper levels of healing. An illness that reveals itself at a superficial level of the body, such as the skin or nose, may represent the resolution of a deeper problem. Just as tears can relieve tension, so the skin can break out in a rash soon after a stressful event. Just how well a condition responds to a natural healing method can depend on exactly where it is lying in this model, and which way it is going. The following table is a simplified version of this model. It should not be used as an absolute guide as Chinese medicine is not as exact a science as Western medicine.

Level	Chinese Term	Western Equivalent	Condition
1.	Taiyang	Skin, mucosal linings	Rash, runny nose, itchy eyes
Superficial			
2.	Shaoyang	Muscles, gall-bladder	Pain syndromes
3.	Yangming	Throat, stomach, bowel	Sore throat, vomiting, diarrhoea
Middle			
4.	Taiyin	Lung, spleen, immune system	Fatigue, immune disorder
5.	Jueyin	Liver, pericardium	Tension, nausea
Deep			
6.	Shaoyin	Kidney/heart	Chronic illness, will

The six energetic layers

The above table demonstrates the principle of depth of *dis-ease*. If you consult a Chinese physician with frequent colds (Levels 1 and 2), he would also 'tonify' your lung and immune system (Level 4) with herbs or acupuncture. Women in early pregnancy suffer, as a rule, more from the misery of constant nausea (Level 5) than vomiting (Level 2).

Shingles is a painful, blistering skin condition, caused by a virus (*Herpes zoster*), which lies dormant in the nerve roots. Older people are particularly at risk, especially after a period of stress has been relieved.

Typically, this would happen, for example, the very day of moving into a retirement apartment.

Similarly the pain of a weekend migraine (Level 3) may signify the 'coming out' of deeply held tensions (Level 5) experienced during the week. Many teachers, for example, present with precisely this pattern. Deep healing will only occur when strategies are adopted dealing with the excessive demands often loaded onto individuals.

These patterns are important for the following reasons:

1. The symptoms often respond well to healing techniques once the diagnosis is confirmed. This is because they already represent a stage of healing. Conditions that respond 'like magic' to one acupuncture treatment are 'ready to heal'.
2. Where the condition occurs can give us a clear indication where the deeper problems lie. Repression, tension, lack of love or joy in the past may all play a part. Talking about these issues or writing them down as we discovered in Chapter 2 may allow further resolution.
3. This information is empowering. Knowing we are on a healing path, and that there are ways to help, can renew our confidence in ourselves.
4. Interventions such as drug treatment or surgery can be minimised. These often do not address the underlying problem. I see many cases where repeated surgery is performed, for continuous pains, when these patterns have not been explored. The result is often a further weakening of the person's resistance.

Debbie's story illustrates this. In many ways, Debbie's plight is similar to that of a teacher who suffers from a headache the moment she relaxes. But with Debbie the roots were deeper and the pains more persistent.

Debbie's story

At last, life was sweet for Debbie. At 32, she had just married Peter after a fairy-tale romance. It had been love at first sight; until then she didn't believe such things could happen.

Debbie was adopted out at birth. Her adoptive parents separated when she was five, and she can still remember the fights they had. From then on she was cared for by her mother, who returned to work, desperately trying to make ends meet. There were three other children but Debbie felt left out — in retrospect, unloved. In her own words, she 'brought herself up', trusting her own instincts without a guide. To this day, she has never met her birth mother.

In her teenage years, she remembers having headaches a few days before heavy, painful periods. She was prescribed the pill for these by her doctor.

In her twenties, Debbie worked as a secretary. She was friendly, outgoing, always willing to listen to other people's problems. There were a few boyfriends, but nobody to whom she felt close. Besides, she enjoyed her independence, understandably wary of any long-term commitment.

Then she met Peter. He was the same age, kind, considerate and a self-employed builder. He designed and built their home into which they moved soon after the wedding.

One month later, Debbie awoke at 2.00 a.m. with severe pains in her side. Peter called the emergency doctor, who gave her a shot of morphine and diagnosed gall-stones. The next day she had a scan, but the results were inconclusive.

The pains returned the next week and then the following week. A decision was made to remove her gall-bladder surgically, through a laparoscope. This was done, revealing a mild degree of inflammation, but no gall-stones. The findings were explained to Debbie with the surgeon hoping this would see an end to her suffering.

Two weeks later the pains returned, and she has continued to get them regularly ever since. It is now two years since her surgery.

Last year Debbie presented with further pains on the same right side, but lower. After scans, she went to surgery, where they discovered endometriosis. Debbie's uterus and both ovaries were removed; she had already decided she didn't want children.

She had just started a course of acupuncture. The doctor who had started her treatment asked her to attend a meeting of holistically minded doctors. There we discussed her case with her to see if we could break this cycle of pain and surgery.

Conclusions

When listening to a story such as Debbie's, it is important that no one makes quick judgements or comes to hasty conclusions. Rather, they should gently explain possible reasons for her continued ill-health, using the mindbody models we have already described.

During the meeting, we talked about Debbie's childhood, her perceived lack of love and her striving for independence. We also discussed her first experience of unconditional love from Peter, her first experience of true happiness. And then the recurrent pain that had interfered with the happy times she so deserved.

We talked of her need to feel in control of the situation, the need to own her healing. She explained she felt a mounting hostility to the doctors and surgeons who, she admitted, were trying their best. Her loss of faith in the medical profession and her frustration with them was making matters even worse.

How does Debbie fit in with the mindbody model?

There is strong evidence emerging that how we perceive the love and caring we receive as children from our parents has a major influence on the diseases we contract in later life. One study followed up the male undergraduates at Harvard University who had participated in the Harvard Mastery of Stress Study in the early 1950s.[51] At that time, they had been asked to describe how loving and caring their parents had been over the preceding 20 years.

Detailed medical and psychological histories were obtained 35 years later. Those who had illnesses such as coronary artery disease, hypertension, duodenal ulcer and alcoholism had used significantly fewer positive words to describe their parents while in college — words such as 'loving', 'friendly', 'warm', 'open', 'understanding', 'sympathetic', and 'just'.

Of those who had given their parents a low 'caring' score as well, 95 percent had these diseases in midlife, compared to only 29 percent of the 'happy' group. The results were independent of other factors such as age, family history, smoking, bereavements and divorce.

We have already seen how repressed feelings can sow the seeds of illness, and that healing can occur from the 'inside out'. In Chinese medicine deep tension causes disharmony in the 'liver' energy. The 'liver' is the vital *zang* organ, and is paired with the less essential *fu* organ, the gall-bladder. According to the Chinese model, previously repressed problems in the liver come to the 'surface' through the gall-bladder, often causing pain. It is likely that Peter's love for Debbie has facilitated this healing.

Unfortunately, the more superficial layers of the body can relay the most pain. Our skin and muscles are highly innervated, protecting our vital organs by giving us painful messages when impacted from the outside. Pain trapped in the more superficial areas may signify a stage of healing, as deeper problems make their way out through the body's armour plating.

Diseases such as coronary artery disease and hypertension have been called the 'silent killers'. These showed up in the Harvard study of men who felt deprived of love as children. The Chinese model would see Debbie's story as one of deep healing — albeit distressing and painful. A necessary exit from the body of the potential causes of these life-threatening illnesses. A freeing-up of repressed thoughts and feelings, a step on the road to potential peace and self-awareness.

꒰ꜱ꒱

Symptom hopping

Our bodies tend to be stubborn and persistent once on the healing trail. Symptoms are not easily quashed by drugs or surgery. Sometimes the body will find another form of 'expression' — a new site for the pain — especially if the target site is removed or suppressed. This also occurs in non-painful conditions; asthma may settle but in its place eczema may erupt on the skin. Irritable bowels calm down only for migraine headaches to re-emerge. 'It's one thing after another, doctor.'

At other times, we will suffer an injury forcing us to look at ourselves and our lives. Think back to the last time you twisted your ankle or sprained your back. What was going on in your life then? Although you may not have admitted it at the time, did you need some 'time out' then? I see this pattern frequently in accident 'victims' who consult me about continuous pain. Going over the story we might find that first the bowels may have 'talked' with pain or loose motions (the autonomic system), then the immune system would have its say with a flu leading to bronchitis and antibiotics.

Next, if ignored by day, the body will start playing up at night — manifesting in insomnia and restlessness. If the body is still not listened to day and night — if the only course of action is taking tranquillisers and sleeping pills — it seems to recruit outside help. It places its foot down that pothole or even finds itself in a car in the wrong lane of a motorway!

꒰ꜱ꒱

The role of acupuncture

If a needle in the hand cured a toothache, that was sufficient for Chinese Taoism. For Western medicine acupuncture was impossible and hence was relegated to the waste-bucket of placebo effects.

— PROFESSOR BRUCE POMERANZ, *BASICS OF ACUPUNCTURE*[52]

The Chinese system of medicine has been practised for over 3000 years, and only recently been subjected to scientific scrutiny. The modern Chinese accept these scientific advances, and are keen to see both Eastern and Western medicine practised side by side. Although there are some die-hard traditionalists, they see Chinese medicine as a dynamic, evolving discipline that must meet standards of quality demanded by an increasingly informed public.

Despite the advances made by modern science in the understanding of acupuncture, we still rely on ancient Chinese wisdom for our treatment plans. Their meridian maps still serve as our guides.

Chinese named most of their meridians after the *zang* and the *fu* organs — i.e., the spleen meridian, the stomach meridian. According to Chinese tradition, in the state of perfect health *qi* flows evenly through all the meridians, which interconnect, and connect the organs to the outside world. Symptoms such as pain represent a block in the flow of *qi* somewhere in a meridian.

Acupuncturists are aware of all these links, and learn to read the signs of disharmony in someone who is unwell. They listen to the voice, observe the colour of the skin, study the tongue and feel the pulses.

They then try to re-establish these links by using needles (as conducting instruments), moxibustion (conducting heat), or their hands (acupressure and massage).

An acupuncturist is rather like a plumber called to a large hotel by a hassled manager. The guests are all complaining about the water in their rooms. For some it is scalding hot, for others freezing cold. Some have no water at all. The plumber has to study the room map, the source (the mains), and the plumbing to the individual rooms — just as an acupuncturist has to recall his anatomy and the meridan lines on the body.

The plumber then asks himself certain questions. Are those with the very hot water inadvertently contributing to the freezing cold water in the other rooms? Is there a problem in the mains supply? Hopefully he has come across this problem before, and can act quickly; or else he treads cautiously, turning some taps on, and others down, watching the response.

He may even fix the problem with one simple twist of a mysterious hidden tap, gaining instant fame and respect. However, he may discover that the plumbing is old and faulty. He can only do so much.

Acupuncturists' lives are filled with similar highs and lows, as they try to help their patients return to a state of balance. But unlike buildings, bodies are dynamic — changing every second. Western medicine has given us detailed insights into the pathology of diseases. We have a fair idea when irreversible damage is done to the body. In these states, acupuncture can be used to create the best environment possible for healing, easing symptoms but not curing the problem. Pain from severe osteoarthritis of the knee or hip is one such example.

However, those who present at an advanced stage of healing can respond rapidly to acupuncture. According to Chinese medicine someone who suffers from pains that skip around his or her body, never settling for long in one place, is showing signs of a *wind* disorder. In Western medicine we don't like to treat this type of problem; we find it confusing when symptoms hop from one place to the next with little respect for the anatomical boundaries we slaved so hard to learn.

The Chinese associate the wind with the liver and the gall-bladder. In a cold wind we tend to wear scarves or turn up the back of our collars to protect ourselves. A 'cold' in Chinese medicine results from a 'cold-wind invasion' at this very part of the body. As it is, there is a pair of acupuncture points on the gall-bladder meridian at the base of our skull. The Chinese name is *feng-chi* or wind tunnel.

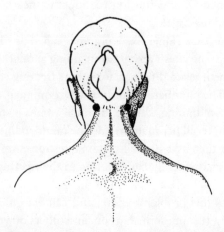

The wind tunnel (acupuncture points gall-bladder 20 *fengchi*)

We can make use of this tunnel to let the 'wind out' by inserting an acupuncture needle into one or both of these points. This can result in relief from the symptoms of a cold, or release of pains which move around the body.

This 'exit point' is also used when tension rises in the body but can't escape through its usual channels. This can occur, for example, when we are unable to express our anger and frustration through words or tears. Liver *qi* rises like hot air compressed in our heads, causing pain and dizziness.

It was simple techniques like this that first drew me to the art of acupuncture and the wisdom of Chinese medicine. In 25 years — one generation — we have started to take this ancient healing art seriously. As old prejudices die, a new generation of scientists from the East and the West have set out to investigate dimensions of the human body known to the Chinese for centuries. This research is being done with a tiny fraction of the research funds granted to pharmaceutical products. Following detailed scrutiny from the US National Institute of Health Consensus in 1997,[53] *Time* magazine ran an article under the headline 'Acupuncture Works'.[54] There were proven advantages shown in using acupuncture to alleviate such conditions as nausea and vomiting after surgery and chemotherapy, and post-operative dental pain.

In addition, NIH saw a useful complementary role in many other conditions — addictions, strokes, fibromyalgia, arthritis and chronic pain. They felt that further research was 'likely to uncover additional areas where acupuncture interventions will be useful'.

Earlier that year the US Food and Drug Administration had removed acupuncture needles from the category of 'experimental medical devices', regulating them with the same vigour as it does with surgical scalpels and syringes. Acupuncture's progress into the 'mainstream' began in the early 1970s, and around the time James Reston received his acupuncture in China. It was discovered that electro-acupuncture — an alternating current machine with leads clipped onto pairs of needles — promoted the production of the body's natural painkiller, the morphine-like endorphins.

These chemicals play a vital role not only in lessening pain but in setting into action many other chemicals vital to healing. In addition, increased levels of other chemicals — serotonin, cortisol, etc. — had been demonstrated. So scientists could measure acupuncture in terms they could understand.

Despite this important validation, 'orthodox' medicine still struggles with the philosophies of Chinese medicine and concepts such as *qi*. Canadian neuroscientist Professor Bruce Pomeranz pioneered the early research into the link between acupuncture and the endorphins. He is one of the many now who advocate a shift away from the narrow thinking that tries to explain the healing arts in solely chemical terms.

We now know that it is not only the body's chemistry that alters when a needle is placed in an acupuncture point. The electrical charge of the skin noticeably changes. The resistance is reduced, and an electrical current can be measured to travel along lines of reduced resistance — from point to point. Sophisticated equipment can now detect these tiny currents and the equally small electromagnetic fields that surround them.

Research is still in its infancy in this area. It will be some time before we have proof that the complex web of meridians represent channels of electromagnetism. Dr Marc Cohen at Monash University, Melbourne, is one Western scientist who has started to investigate this hypothesis. His team is interested in whether the traditional acupuncture points and their connecting channels, the meridians, are important in conducting information in our bodies.

His findings suggest that:[55]

1. Energy, in the form of electromagnetic waves, can be transmitted from one point on a meridian to another, in the way traditionally described by the Chinese.
2. The pattern of frequencies transmitted (8–45 Hz) closely matches the Schumann Resonances (see page 153). The dominant Schumann Resonance of 8 Hz, in turn, matches the state recorded in our brains by an EEG monitor when we are most relaxed or in a meditative state.

    This work suggests that our outside environment, our acupuncture meridians, and our central nervous system *resonate* to produce a state within our bodies that promotes healing.
3. Acupuncture points are likely to represent areas on the body where there is a 'freer flow' of information between the inside and the outside of the body. The electrical resistance has been shown to be lower at acupuncture points and along the meridians.[56, 57]

Another theory links the course of the Chinese meridians with bands of connective tissue, known as fascial layers. These have been regarded as merely mechanical barriers and protective sheaths coating our muscles. However, they may have another interesting physical property: they are comprised of collagen fibres that bind water molecules. Water is known to be a very efficient conductor of these frequencies.

Connecting to the outside world — the Schumann Resonances[57]

Every second there are about 100 lightning strikes around the world. About 80 percent of these occur over the world's three main tropical rainforest areas — South-east Asia, sub-Sahara Africa and the Amazon Basin. Thunderstorm activity is greatest in the late afternoons but because these areas are evenly spaced around the world, a constant level of activity is maintained.[59]

This leads to electromagnetic activity between the earth and the ionosphere that, in turn, produces the Schumann Resonances (8–45 Hz). The dominant component is around 8 Hz which also corresponds to alpha wave frequencies recorded on an EEG when we are in a relaxed or meditative state.

It is interesting to speculate that healing practices such as meditation and acupuncture involve tuning into these life-enhancing vibrations. And that the healer acts as a transmitter or channeller of these healing frequencies when performing a healing practice, such as therapeutic touch, on another.

So we seem to be unravelling evidence of new, vital connections with our world, and the cosmos. In the coming century, this may prove as important to our planet's health as our understanding of the air we breathe and the food we eat.

For a therapist and health professional, acupuncture is a marvellous tool with which to facilitate healing. It allows me to get close to and actually communicate tactilely with the physical messages we have talked about at length. Symptoms such as pain, fatigue and sadness are in essence not verbal — we simply try to explain them to others in these terms. They are often incredibly difficult to express with words.

One of the most accurate ways to describe pain is by using our hands. We automatically straighten our fingers to imitate a knife when describ-

ing sharp stabbing pain; we form a closed fist to indicate a stuck, gnawing
constant pain. We open and close our fist to describe cramping, 'collicky'
pains of gall-stones.

For me, it is first important to hear the person's own story, told his or
her way. Then, I tune in directly to the body, opening up a conversation
in its own language. The acupuncture needle is merely a conductor of
this information from the inside of the body to the outside. And the acupuncture points are simply specific areas of exchange of this information,
discovered by many people over many years. They are, according to
Chinese medicine, where the internal organs, both the vital *zang* and
their paired *fu*, communicate with the outside world; where information
'enters' and where it 'escapes'.

The acupuncture needle is, therefore, like an aerial, picking up and
transmitting messages in the form of different frequencies. The Chinese

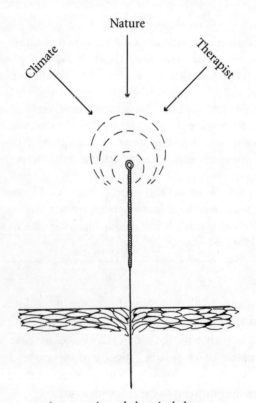

Autonomic and chemical changes

The acupuncture needle as a transmitting aerial

advise against performing acupuncture when an electrical storm is raging outside. It is essential that it is done in an atmosphere of peace and tranquillity, and this is one reason doctors find it difficult to practise it in a hectic, general practice setting. As the figure on page 154 shows, the 'blunt end' and the 'sharp end' of the needle are of equal importance.

Transmitting a signal may not even depend on the use of a needle. Children, in particular, frequently report 'tickly feelings' when acupuncture points are lightly touched. Without any prior knowledge of Chinese medicine, it is not unusual for a child to describe in detail these sensations travelling along a known acupuncture meridian.

Try this simple exercise on your child, partner or close friend.

Simple meridian exercise

1. Relax with your child or partner. Sharing a joke is a great way to 'harmonise' with them.
2. Hold one of your hands out and focus your attention on it. Be patient. After a time you will probably become aware of a gentle warm tingling in the hand.
3. Now move your attention to the tip of the longest, middle finger.
4. If this is warm and tingling (it is sometimes very subtle), rest the tip lightly on your partner's or child's wrist, five centimetres — about three finger breadths — above the wrist on the inner (palm) side (see figure below).
5. Remain relaxed and patient.

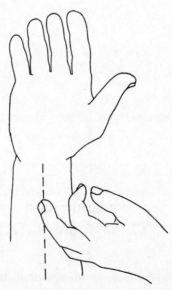

Location of point on the heart protector (pericardium) meridian (PC 6)

Responses

1. The extremely sensitive will trace a line from the point up their arm into their chest. Children under 11 often report this. This corresponds to the meridian, or channel, known in Chinese medicine as the *pericardium* or *heart protector*.
2. A typical response, once both parties are relaxed and confident, is to note a tingling sensation travelling up towards the elbow.
3. If there is no response, swap roles. Often, one person will have a more sensitive system than the other. Then swap back; you may find it easier the second time.

The figure below shows how this exercise allows two heart protector channels to join. The same happens when two people hold hands — when the palms join.

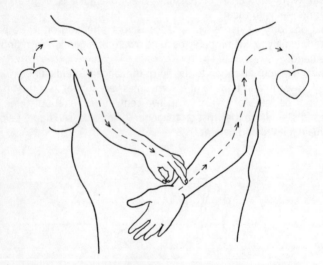

Heart to heart: energy transfer from healer to healee

The healing path

The teacher opens the door, but you must enter by yourself.

— CHINESE PROVERB

The role of the healer is to facilitate an optimum state of healing, combining skill, wisdom and compassion. The healing arts assist the healer.

Acupuncture uses needles to conduct a state of harmony and connection in the body but only after the body is listened to. A dialogue commences with a pattern of signs and symptoms answered by a pattern of needles at various parts of the body. Each time the body is listened to, its dynamic state is honoured. A homoeopathic practitioner will enter into a similar dialogue — the symptoms answered this time with matching remedies.

This state is known as *physiological relearning*. The body is remembering how to be well again. This is the same as any learning process. When we first try to ride a bike, it can seem impossible. But we persist, practising day-in day-out. Then all of a sudden with a slight wobble we're off. A week later, we hop on and disappear up the road. It all seems so easy. Of course, it also depends on two factors: we have to have the will to persist, and the belief we can do it.

The aim of the healer, like the teacher, is to set the process in motion — to open the door. The word 'doctor' is derived from the Latin verb *docere* — to teach. To heal is to achieve a state of internal peace and wellness, a sense of self in harmony with one's surroundings. The symptoms of all chronic illnesses fluctuate in a chaotic manner. At their worst, there seems little the sufferer can do to influence this pattern. Even when on a healing path, progress can seem frustratingly slow. Two steps forward, one step back.

M	T	W	T	F	S	S
			1	2	✕ 3	4
5	6	✕ 7	8	9	10	11
12	13	14	✕ 15	16	✕ 17	18
19	20	21	✕ 22	23	24	✕ 25
26	✕ 27	28	✕ 29	30	✕ 31	

✕ = Pain-free or fatigue-free days

Calendar marked by patient showing 'well' days

But healing is a dynamic, natural process. We must look, like the Eastern physicians, to nature for insights; to the unfolding of the seasons, or to the progression of an incoming tide on a beach:

When winter turns to spring, not every day is warmer or finer than
the day before.
   When the tide comes in, not every wave advances further than the
one before.

Healing from a long-standing illness progresses in a similar way. A
good day is followed by a 'not so good' day. But month by month, then
week by week, the number of good days increases. There may then be
two good days joined, then three. In our first story, Ruby experienced a
fleeting moment, several seconds, free of pain after many years. This was
to herald the start of a healing journey.

As children, our teachers continually warned us to be patient. They
were there to give us the 'big picture', encouraging us in the learning
process. The most difficult lesson is first learning how to be well again.
Most will feel uneasy during their first pain-free day, but will be unwilling to mention this to anyone for fear of sounding ungrateful. I raise
the subject myself when talking to someone in the early stages of healing;
this seems to have a reassuring effect.

Inevitably, people in this situation start scurrying around, shopping,
buying presents, spring-cleaning and doing all those odd jobs around the
house. The result — total collapse and relapse. This is a human tendency,
and it happens every time. The clinical psychologist Dr William Collinge
advocates the 50 percent solution to all those recovering from Chronic
Fatigue Syndrome:[60]

1. Plan your well days by making a list of what you hope to achieve.
2. Then cross out half the activities. The energy you were to use for
   these deleted tasks should be invested in your own healing.

I find 50 percent rather conservative. I often have to go to stage 2 —
halve the 50 percent to 25 percent! This is a time when an old-fashioned
teacher is needed.

As the patient learns this discipline, more control is taken on. More
owning of the healing. The symptoms are seen to respond favourably to
these actions. Whereas previously chaos ruled, order and control return.

A healing art such as acupuncture can also help 'rescue' someone in a
relapse. The dips shown in the graph on page 159 do not sink so low. At
the same time, the 25–50 percent solution can be reinforced. Self-healing
exercises such as breathing and meditation can be taught; the patient
learns to *be* as well as to *do*.

Whereas pain and fatigue lead to muddled thoughts and apathy, a state of wellness leads to a state of clarity. New insights are gained, often subconsciously. The deep emotional scars of the past are acknowledged and the barriers to healing are identified. Old friends are contacted and new ones made. It is often a time for forgiveness.

The combined effect of all this is seen as the turning point in the graph below.

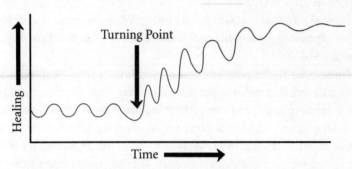

The Healing Pattern (after Dr W. Collinge)

As healing progresses, thoughts can turn to helping and healing others — joining a group, helping with its running, working as a volunteer at a hospice, etc. As long as the 50 percent rule is observed, this wounded healer role has added benefits to the patient.

Portia reflects on this in *The Merchant of Venice*:

> The quality of mercy is not strained,
> It droppeth as the gentle rain from heaven
> Upon the place beneath; it is twice blessed;
> It blesseth him that gives, and him that takes.

The doctor/healer/teacher is a guide; ideally, as healing progresses, techniques such as acupuncture can be phased out in preference to the self-help measures described in Chapters 3 and 8. In practice, patients are happy to know that there is a therapy available as a 'back-up'. And a friendly ear that listens.

Healing times

Although I have described a consistent pattern, the time taken to heal varies considerably. In general, the longer the illness has been present, the longer and more haphazard the recovery course. A simple cut will fully heal in 10 days if there is no infection and the edges are taped closely together. However, if the wound is deep and open, it will take several weeks for the wound to heal from the base upwards. Ruptured ligaments may take three months, with frozen shoulders often causing pain and restriction for a year and a half.

These are examples of structural healing. What about the deeper levels of healing that involve many complex issues as well as the discovery of a new sense of self?

Think back to the last time you moved home. How long did it take for you to feel that this was indeed your place? That you fitted in to the new neighbourhood, and stopped pining for your old house despite all its inadequacies. Moving is stressful; apart from all the hassles with furniture, estate agents and lawyers, it's like losing an old friend even if you are gaining a new, possibly better one. My own experiences, and those of many patients who find themselves surprised at the stress and grief of moving, suggest that it takes a full 18 months. Deep healing can be seen in a similar light.

Once we have identified the reasons why healing has been blocked, I usually suggest that it is going to take about 18 months at least, especially if the 'build up' has been over a lifetime. Often, it is clear that we have inherited unresolved issues from previous generations, so it could be said that we are seeing the after-effects of many lifetimes.

The length of time healing takes can prove difficult. Modern medicine strives to produce new drugs that produce their effects swiftly and conveniently. They are marketed slickly and attractively — just think of 'Quick-ease'. Even natural products, such as the many vitamin and mineral supplements that abound, are heavily promoted by large multi-national companies with only scant reference to the length of time it takes to see results.

But most of the people I see are the 'chronically ill'. They are still ill despite the latest wonder drug and super vitamin. Modern commercial medicine has not provided the answer or the cure for them. Nor has the system provided the time to reflect on their healing potential as each therapist forlornly tries out one possible new cure after another, ending up as lost and frustrated as their patient.

But it gets better. Even though the healing course is long and jagged, it does actually begin. Together we analyse the signs. The good day 'out of the blue'. Feeling a bit different. Starting to sing in the shower. And each time we say it will get better still.

So what are the conditions we are talking about?

Our stories have revealed a wide range of conditions that have improved 'against the odds'. Our standard medical terminology is limited when we talk of healing; conditions are cured but it is people who heal. My job is to assess a person's potential to heal; the blocks we can identify, the will, the patterns, the overload on the defence system at the time of onset. Often we need to turn the clock back.

At the same time we have to be sensible. Many conditions are programmed into us on our DNA. We inherit the tendency to get migraine headaches but these may only emerge when our internal environment becomes imbalanced — at times of 'stress' or changes in our bodies such as menopause. When this happens, the healing does not *cure* the person of the underlying problem — in many ways everything else is sorted out so that the migraines do not take hold. The teacher with the weekend migraine identifies the tensions of the week, both inside and outside the classroom. She may also receive acupuncture, noticing that although the headache starts on a Friday, it isn't as severe. She takes some paracetamol and is surprised when she wakes with only mild pain in the morning. By Sunday she is headache free. Two weeks later she does get a 'real boomer', oddly enough in the middle of the week. By the next day it's gone. Then, no more headaches for three weeks.

After six weeks, she sees that the pattern is broken; that when the migraines do come, they are usually milder. They can still come out of the blue but she has now 'got her life back'. There is a tremendous difference between a migraine a week, and a migraine a month.

Identifying who can be healed is a highly controversial area. Health fraud is widespread, and watchdog groups keenly scan their domains for quacks and fraudsters who take advantage of the weak and vulnerable. They are also hard on 'fringe' professions who hide behind 'pseudo-scientific' data to justify their treatments. On the other hand, there is a growing tendency to treat *evidence-based data* as the only valid measure of effective healthcare. Evidence-based medicine does not talk of healing. It doesn't talk of professional skill levels, whether they are homoeo-paths, bodyworkers or surgeons. By and large it sees our bodies as isolated units of tissue that can be acted on by defined protocols to produce measurable results. Impersonal and, by design, unemotional.

There are dangers with this approach too. The opposite to the placebo response can occur — the *nocebo*. When people are given chemically inactive pills as part of a clinical trial, a certain number will show a clinical improvement — the placebo response. A number, however, will experience unpleasant side effects even though there is no obvious chemical in the compound. It has even been discovered that competitive and aggressive subjects are more likely to suffer these nocebo effects than mild-mannered individuals.[61]

When inactive sterile water is injected 'blindly' into subjects with chronic pain, a percentage will be relieved of their pain. In fact, it is now known that their own chemicals change — their opioids (the endorphins) are activated. Another chemical — naloxone — has even been shown to block this response by antagonising the natural endorphins.[62]

So the powers of suggestion can have major effects on our symptoms and our chemistry. Recently I attended a review at the local offices of our New Zealand Accident Compensation Commission. Similar scenes are enacted daily in workers' compensation cases worldwide. I was with Brian, a 26-year-old university lecturer who had been seeing me for several weeks with chronic pain in his arms. The university had undergone staff cutbacks, and the lecturers were trying to cope with large amounts of computer and paperwork. At the onset of pain, a full year earlier, Brian's father had died — he had not seen him for years, and he ended up looking after him at his home for two weeks. As well as administering painkillers and co-ordinating his care, Brian addressed and resolved many issues with his father who until that time had been a distant figure.

Less than two years earlier, Brian had nursed his mother who was dying of terminal cancer. He had then gone straight back to the pressure of his qualifying exams.

Brian asked me to support him at the interview; he feared they would cut his benefit, forcing him back to work just as he felt he was healing. I agreed that sending him back too early would be unwise.

As I sat down, I was surprised by the case manager's opening request to me: 'Doctor, tell Brian that he will never be pain free. That if he gets back to work, he will have something to take his mind off it.'

They seemed equally surprised when I disagreed. I said that he was improving, and that we were exploring the issues that were delaying his healing. They produced statistics to support their case that he had an 'incurable condition', remarking that grief was not classified as an accident in their set of rules.

Nevertheless, we won a reprieve for three months with a further improvement of Brian's pain for our efforts.

Funding authorities are not involved in healing. To them either a condition is curable, with evidence available to that effect, or incurable. They will fund the cheapest and most effective therapy, even if this only addresses the symptoms. They deal in numbers and dollars. If an accident insurance company hears that grief could be involved, they will query their right to recompense an injury. They live by their own black and white rules, written in their rule book.

Healing involves individuals in unique circumstances. By branding someone unhealable, authority figures can be the proclaimers of a self-fulfilling prophecy — a powerful nocebo. It is certainly the right of all 'patients' to be made aware of any statistics that relate to their conditions. However, their importance has to be kept firmly in perspective.

What conditions respond best to healing?

Traditionally, conditions that do not manifest with measurable changes in the tissues have been labelled *functional*. By and large, these conditions are transient and not life-threatening, although they can cause untold misery and suffering. Examples include irritable bowel syndrome, migraines, premenstrual syndrome, chronic pain and fatigue states. Sufferers from these 'syndromes' now regularly seek out healing practitioners for alternative or complementary care. Some have tried orthodox medicine with poor results; a growing number are unhappy even to start medication because of deeply held concerns about side-effects and the limits of 'just treating the symptoms'. They are keen to be part of the healing process, thereby maintaining a sense of control. This time, the positive attitude pays off and the healing itself becomes part of this self-fulfilling prophecy.

Tradition labels all the other measurable conditions as *organic*. These are illnesses with firm diagnoses derived from scientifically based, recordable data using blood tests, X-rays, biopsies, MRI scans, etc. Such illnesses include cancer, coronary artery disease, diabetes mellitus and rheumatoid arthritis. Treatment is usually chemically or surgically based with social and psychological approaches taking their place firmly in supporting roles. To be fair, the move to incorporate this 'psycho-social' paradigm has been a feature of the more holistic approach that has filtered into orthodox medicine in the late twentieth century. It has been fuelled by public awareness and also by the landmark studies quoted in this book.

Just how far we have progressed in this integrative approach was brought home to me recently on reading a contemporary review of a famous heart study, first published in 1982.

The Beta-Blocker Heart Attack Trial showed that we could reduce the chances of heart patients dying by prescribing the beta-blocking drug propranolol to those who had already suffered a heart attack.[63] Overall mortality was reduced by 26 percent, which was significant enough for the medical profession, myself included, to recommend this line of treatment with some enthusiasm. However, further analysis subsequently showed that those men who were both socially isolated and lived with 'high stress levels' — about a fifth of the study group — were more than four times at risk of dying than other men.[64]

I cannot remember being aware of this 'heart-mind' data at the time, and maybe its significance would have been lost on me then. At that time the common assumption was that our effectiveness as doctors lay as prescribers first and advisers second. A patient's social context was given only secondary consideration, even if lifestyle was seen as contributing to certain diseases.

I continue to believe that the role of medication should be put in context, and that the doctor should discuss with each patient issues that continue to put him at risk. A patient's social isolation is a risk factor that can be clearly identified. It involves issues of love, companionship, and even how he relates to the community at large. It may even suggest that the relationship struck up between the doctor and the patient can have a direct bearing on the patient's healing. Maybe, a trusting friendship is the best medicine.

Prescribing a drug such as propranolol has, no doubt, saved many lives. Drugs are hugely important in the management of heart disease. But we can now begin to view the big picture. We are seeing the 'medicalisation' of illnesses in the context of a much broader canvas; for doctors this means releasing some of the control we have wielded in the past. Information and responsibility have to be shared and the healing value of relationships taken seriously.

So the margins between *functional* and *organic* illness are now increasingly blurred. Whenever two humans interact with noble intent, as in any health professional consultation, there is healing.

When prescribing medication or giving advice to their patients, Tibetan doctors traditionally complement their treatments with the word 'Mettā'. Translated this means 'With loving kindness'.

A powerful placebo delivered from the heart.

10. Modern theories

Healing in proportion

We don't know a millionth of one percent of anything.
— Thomas Edison, 1847–1931

I don't intend to blind you with science. I have not dedicated my life to the pursuit of scientific theory; I rely, like most doctors, on the wise teachings of those scientists who have the intelligence, discipline and passion to advance the frontiers of human knowledge. The scientist's journey can be frustratingly, painstakingly slow — a meticulous art whose practitioners I admire but do not envy. A doctor's life could not be further removed from this. Every new patient throws up a new challenge every few minutes, and the doctor must balance safety with efficiency, knowledge with compassion. We quickly acknowledge that the answers don't all come from the pages of our textbooks. I have never seen two people completely alike — not even identical twins. Nor are two conditions ever alike; every backache or sore throat is unique.

If general practice makes doctors experts in anything, it is in relationships. How ill health relates to people's lives. How they relate to each other, and the outside world. It was this that first attracted me to the world of Eastern medicine with its huge data base of observations and understanding about humanity. I suspect this has drawn me to the insights of poets, the succinct observers and recorders of the human condition.

The poet sees not deep, but wide.
— Matthew Arnold

A doctor, like a poet, has to be vigilant and aware, conveying simple messages back to a confused public. Someone who has somehow had a peek at the big picture, and can see our problems for what they really are — in true proportion.

I have had to search further still in my quest to gain some sense of proportion to the subject of healing. Doctors and psychologists are only starting to study what exactly it is that constitutes a healing relationship. For me this has meant 'getting back to the scientific drawing board' — to the world of atoms and that which lies within.

The simple atom

Let's start with proportions. We'll use as our example the simplest, smallest known atom — the hydrogen atom. Now look at the following dash: –. We could fit 20 million hydrogen atoms into this dash — more atoms than there are people in New York City, Greater London and New Zealand combined.[65]

Atoms combine to form molecules. For example, two hydrogen atoms combine with an oxygen atom to form a water molecule, H_2O. We are used to seeing models of these molecules represented by different coloured balls, like little billiard balls, bound to each other with sticks. We could be forgiven for thinking that this image is an accurate scaled-up version of the real thing.

Yet, if we venture inside the atomic billiard ball, we get another surprise. It is not solid at all. In fact, it has a nucleus in the middle, and an electron whirling around it, orbiting in space.

So we literally get back to the drawing board, to the way this is classically represented (see below).

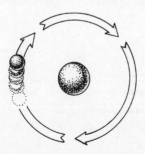

Hydrogen atom with single electron in orbit around single nucleus (proton)

With this representation, the electron is rotating in orbit yet there is something very wrong even with this picture. Like the molecular model, it is designed within the limitations of the medium we are using. If we drew this true to scale, this book would have to be over half a kilometre wide, as the true distance between the electron's orbit and the nucleus would be 500 metres![65]

So now we have to imagine the scene in virtual reality, rather like we are travelling from a planet to the sun surrounded by vast spaces of nothingness.

But we are still making assumptions. Assumptions that these sub-atomic particles are like balls or bits. If we think that's the whole story, we are nearly a century behind the times. Again this has been just a convenient image based on the tangible world we have been safe in. The world we can touch and see and make sense of. Closer to reality would be to 'see' these particles — the electrons — as wave-forms. Like a hazy blur of light or a puff of smoke.

It was the scientist Louis de Broglie who in 1924 first suggested this phenomenon — the wave/particle duality. Subsequent experiments have shown this indeed to be true.

One practical development of this discovery has been the electron microscope, which uses electron 'waves' instead of light waves.

This was the birth of quantum physics, which developed on the back of Albert Einstein's theory that matter and energy are both aspects of the same reality. The next step was to take the whole debate out 'of sight' and even out of imagination, into the area of mathematics, statistics and probabilities. This has produced more startling revelations.

The electrons, quantum science has determined, come and go in and out of existence. They can be seen to exist as probabilities, particles or quanta of excitation, materialising and dematerialising in relatively vast fields.

To recap:

We are made of cells

That are made of molecules

That are made of atoms,

Which are made of 'vast' fields

in which you find tiny particles

That are really waves

That come and go.

As this picture was unfolding in the early twentieth century, physicist Sir Arthur Eddington summed it up by saying that it seemed 'the stuff of the world is mind stuff'.

Information

> What we observe is not nature itself, but nature exposed to our method of questioning.
>
> — WERNER HEISENBERG, QUANTUM PHYSICIST

We have gone through this journey into inner space using our senses and imagination to grapple with some of these concepts. We have formed images in our mind, still life and movies, and possibly recalled pulling apart the models of molecules while our chemistry teacher was out of the room. Some of us will have worked out that 500 metres is the length of that tricky par-5 hole on the golf course. And we have ended up rather frustrated and powerless that these impossibly clever mathematicians have come up with all the answers in a way we'll never understand.

What we really have been doing is processing information.

Symptoms are our body's information. If you are unfortunate enough to break your leg, a nurse or doctor may ask you to describe the degree of pain you are suffering. There is in common usage a Visual Analogue Scale (VAS) which measures pain 'as a score' out of 10 — with 10 out of 10 being the worst pain imaginable. It is likely that you would score your broken leg close to this. If your pet dog was to suffer the same fate, he would likely be experiencing the same degree of misery but we would not be able to get the information from him in such an understandable form. However, the pure information, pain, is the same.

Similarly, we may be able to measure chemicals in the blood that rise in response to pain, but they are not the pain itself. The 'molecules of emotion' measured by Candace Pert and Michael Ruff are not the emotions themselves but simply a measurable by-product of the emotions. Emotions, pain and symptoms are examples of pure *quantum information*, which we try to make sense of using simple analogue and digital scales of measurement. Our brains, in fact, can be seen as highly sophisticated computers that do this very thing, un-scrambling the chaos of all this quantum information.

When we apply such logic to all phenomena, we start to realise that information may be more fundamental than mass and even energy. As Heisenberg implied: what we perceive as 'reality' is 'true reality' exposed to our methods of questioning. Whether something is large or small, heavy or light depends on how finely tuned are our senses and our own subjective experience of life.

Cushion exercise
1. Find a cushion — one from the living room sofa will do.
2. Pick it up and describe to yourself how it feels — is it soft or hard, smooth or textured?
3. Now imagine you are a fly landing on the cushion. How does it feel to your now flylike feet?
4. Imagine that you are an elephant with one foot on the cushion. How does the cushion feel?

The cushion is only soft to humans because of our particular sense of touch. The property of softness is not transferable to all members of the animal kingdom. Our perception of reality is limited to our senses, our connections to the outside world. The cushion may be red, but a dog with its monochrome vision doesn't know this.

Now ask a family member to hide the cushion. *Does the cushion now even exist?*

Everything is relative. The cushion holds all the relevant information, which we then convert for our own use. Information is fundamental.

We live in the information age. Telephones, cellular networks, facsimile machines, e-mail, the internet. All these involve the transmission of classical information to our eyes and ears, and even touch through pagers that vibrate in our pockets. This works on a binary system — a sophisticated, superfast Morse Code of dots and dashes deciphered by computers and converted into the written word, sound or video. But the transfer of information within our bodies, and between us, appears to be more sophisticated. The human/machine experiments suggest that this transfer of information has special qualities. It occurs instantly and is enchanced by human caring. So living systems seem to have another dimension to their communication that technology is, as yet, unable to match. We may be able to fax or e-mail two-dimensional letters and photos around the world, but not cakes, socks or ourselves (outside *Star Trek*).

So what has all this to do with healing? We have talked about symptoms being the bodymind's information, which we convert often rather ineptly into words. We have seen that healing can occur when this pure information is listened to and purely interpreted by ourselves, assisted at times by a surrogate healer. We have seen from the stories and studies the healing value of bonds of unconditional friendship and love.

How close has science come to understanding these bonds?

Entanglement — electronic friendship

We must now take a trip back to our hydrogen atom. Our electron — we'll call her 'Blur' — is spinning in and out of existence in what is now called a state of 'superposition'. As soon as we start to observe 'Blur', she settles into a definite spin — either up or down. But 'Blur' has a friend, a buddy out there. They have a pure bond together known as *entanglement*. As soon as 'Blur' starts spinning clockwise, her friend 'Anti-Blur' spins anti-clockwise (see below).

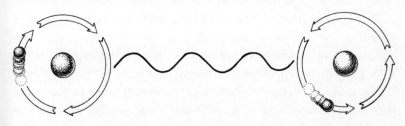

'Entanglement' bonds between two electrons.
Note: Electron on left spins clockwise; electron on right spins anti-clockwise

And this is where it gets rather interesting. It makes no difference whether the gap between electrons is a few centimetres or many kilometres, entanglement is independent of distance. Scientists from the University of Geneva set out to investigate this in 1997. Dr Nicolas Gisin and colleagues sent 'entangled' pairs of photons — waves/particles of light — down fibre-optic cables to detectors 10 kilometres apart. They found that the measurement of one photon *instantaneously* influenced the result of the other.[66]

The next question to be asked was whether this is just some odd, isolated finding, or does entanglement represent the way all electrons and atoms relate to each other? Do all our electrons have this amazing gift of communicating with each other, irrespective of the distance between them?

Physicist Sandu Popescu, together with mathematician Noah Linden of Cambridge University, are discovering that these links also occur in groups of particles.[67] In fact, in the 'quantum state' these non-local bonds seem to be the rule, not the exception. It is beginning to appear that there are connections between the atoms of all things, including ourselves, that know no barriers in time or space.

This scene draws remarkable parallels with the findings of the PEAR team in Princeton, which we examined in Chapter 4. These revealed that the human mind can influence the output of certain machines independent of time and space. This can happen from distances of thousands of kilometres, and can be enhanced by couples working together in harmonious relationships. There were no human superstars, but the most consistent results were from those people who felt they formed a 'special bond' with their machines.

So we are beginning to find evidence of the ultimate 'open' communication system. The ramifications of this are literally mind-stretching. Applied to our own bodies, we can see a clearer picture of the instant internal network we began to explore in Chapter 7. These entangled bonds have no physical barriers and need not be restricted to any anatomical organ, or by our skin, explaining some of the 'trans-personal' phenomena we have discussed. It also possibly explains how one human being can open another up to healing.

And because this network is all encompassing, we can begin to gain perspective on our attempts to 'connect' with nature. The breathing exercises, meditation, and mindfulness all honour the principle that none of us live in isolation.

To quote journalist Mark Buchanan of *The New Scientist*:

'. . . the link of entanglement knows no boundaries. It isn't a cord running through space, but lives somehow outside space. It goes through walls, and pays no attention to distance.'[68]

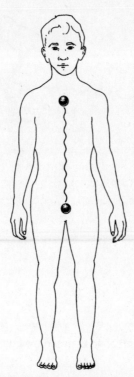

'Entanglement' bond within the body

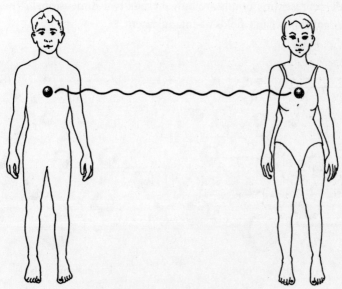

'Entanglement' bond between people

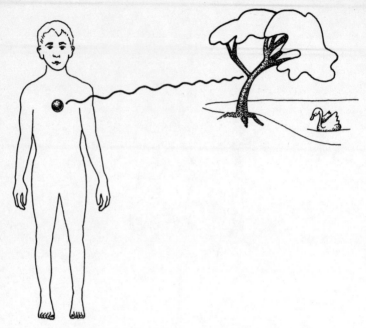

'Entanglement' bond between the body and nature

Again we must bear in mind that these diagrams with their wavy 'cords' representing bonds are only a crude two-dimensional depiction representing invisible fields of entanglement.

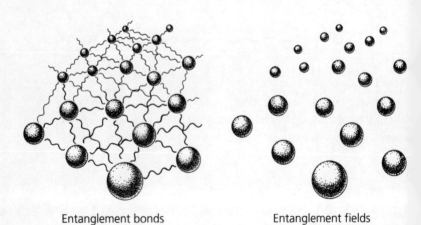

Entanglement bonds   Entanglement fields

Passing on messages

When we have an important message to be passed on to someone, we tend to select a reliable, dependable messenger. The entangled bond is predictable in that when 'Blur' is spinning one way, we know 'Anti-Blur' is doing the exact opposite. Scientists are exploring this reliability, wondering whether it can be used to transport information about a totally different electron (Z) from electron (X) (Blur) and electron (Y) (Anti-Blur). In fact, in the laboratory they have succeeded in doing this using 'single' particles. They call this *quantum teleporting*[69] (see figure below).

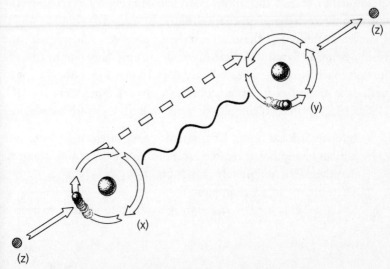

Quantum 'teleporting' of information (about electron z)
via entangled electrons (x and y)

A 'carbon copy' of (Z) is being instantly produced at a distant point with our entangled bond acting as our e-mail network. This phenomenon is interesting communication companies since the potential for a quantum computer, which doesn't depend on deciphering binary codes, is truly limitless. It is possible that the e-mail of today will become the snail mail of tomorrow.

It would also seem that our own brain functions as a hugely complex version of such a quantum computer, making sense of messages that bombard it from all around. It converts chaos into something we can use and understand. In fact, modern-day illnesses such as chronic pain and chronic fatigue states are beginning to be regarded as the result of an overload of data on the brain. The same thing happens on a computer when too many programs are being run.

Professor Jahn's team of researchers at Princeton has also been intrigued by the extrasensory transfer of information from one human being to another.[18] In a complementary set of anomalous experiments, one group of participants, known as *percipients*, extracted details of a remote geographical location, making notes on a standard check sheet and taking pictures of it. They were instructed to immerse themselves 'emotionally and cognitively' in the experience. Meanwhile, at points many miles away, another group, *agents*, paired up to them and attempted to 'receive' this information telepathically. They recorded the 'data' on the same standard check sheet.

Several hundred of these experiments have been studied, with the results being analysed statistically. Trends are emerging that mirror the human/machine interaction studies, and which may even be beginning to define the properties of our relationships with each other, and the world.

Out of a vast mass of complex data, the following picture is emerging:

1. Information can indeed be passed on 'extrasensorily' from one human to another at remote locations. (Statistics strongly suggest that these were not merely chance findings.)
2. There are no 'gifted' champions.
3. Results are enhanced by a *feeling of resonance* between the two people.

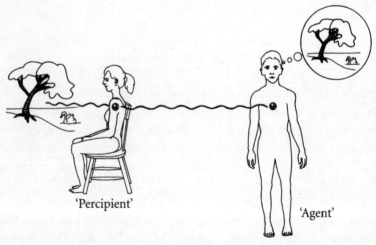

'Percipient'   'Agent'

Remote perception between percipient and agent

4. Results are enhanced by *a feeling of resonance* between the percipient and the environment he or she was immersed in (see figure on facing page).

Although it remains pure speculation at present, it is intriguing to suggest that this model in some way provides a 'blueprint' for healing. It suggests that there are bonds within the body that act as fields to enable information, messages and symptoms to be transmitted instantly to other parts of the body. It suggests that there are bonds between humans and other animals that allow the same free flow of information; bonds between humans and nature. And the behaviour of all the main players in this act is openness, resonance, coherence, immersion, listening, caring, even loving. All are best performed in an ego-free environment, knowing that there are no talented champions.

We can also begin to surmise why and how these bonds become blocked. How we can have within us a confused sense of self, where these bonds are not open. Bodies consumed by worries and past traumas, barriers to the information flow of the 'here and now'. A testament to the times when we have been unable to listen to our 'inner voices'. Alternatively, there could be times when the messages were so frequent and confused that the system became overloaded and clamped up.

The notion of remote perception can be adapted to fit the healer/patient relationship, the basis of traditional healing rituals.

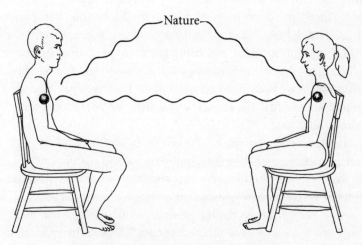

'Entanglement' bond between healer and patient,
sharing a universal bond with nature

The healing ritual

Although initially a modern medical consultation may seem light years away from the mystical behaviour of a shaman, closer scrutiny reveals similarities. True, it is unlikely that your doctor will go to the extremes of slipping into a shamanic trance every time he sees you, but he should be listening to you. The shaman creates in himself an altered state, devoid of rationality and worry, in which he acts as an empty vessel for information — a pure channeller or *percipient*. Similar, but less dramatic, altered states are induced in patients today through hypnotherapy, rebirthing, and even acupuncture. The healing practitioner is, ideally, not removed but part of this state. A true bond of *resonance* can only form between the healer and patient if both are involved.

Common to all healing rituals is the recognition that we are at one with our surroundings — our *universality*. We go out of our way to introduce this issue at the outset of any meeting. We may talk about the weather, an experience that we both share, and can perhaps agree on. Even 'Good day' can be seen as an efficient mixture of heartfelt good intent, and the recognition of an experience shared by all. We then try to secure our own bond with the person, by shaking hands — joining 'hearts' according to the Chinese — and *resonating* as we move our hands up and down together, achieving perfect harmony.

We then try to secure these bonds by exploring common interests, mutual passions, shared friendships. We talk and listen, making each other feel worthy and appreciated. The doctor/healing professional should then listen intently, opening up to the information being presented. Immersing him- or herself in the present as if nothing else mattered.

At this point orthodox and complementary practitioners tend to go their separate ways. The homoeopath and traditional Chinese physician will probe your bodymind relationships. They will pay attention to emotional, spiritual issues, deepening their understanding and their *transpersonal bond*.

The classical homoeopath will then try to match your symptoms, or internal messages, with the corresponding homoeopathic remedy. He or she matches 'like with like', in an act similar to when we repeat back to someone what they have just said, indicating we have been listening. The remedy is prepared from natural products, which through trial and error have been shown to have the best results. Modern interpretations of homoeopathy suggest that harmonic frequencies are matched up — a *resonance* is formed.

Orthodoxy struggles to understand why diluting something progressively in water can produce a remedy that can have any therapeutic effect. However, water, as we have seen, is not simply a dilutant of drugs and chemicals. It is an information transmitter, with each atom able to store and pass on *quantum information*. It surely is within the realms of possibility that 'pure' information can be stored in the memory data bank of this unique combination of hydrogen and oxygen atoms that makes up a single molecule of water.

The complementary healer may then go a step further. For example, Chinese physicians then 'listen' with their fingers, receiving information about the body's imbalances through feeling the pulses. Touching is a two-way process, and this is another chance for two humans to resonate. As doctors, we can lose sight of how important simple touch is for patients. Many, especially men, are starved of touch; it is regrettable that medical-legal issues surrounding touch make many practitioners wary of touching their patients. Psychologists, in particular, are now denied this valuable healing tool. Valuable to both partners of a healing relationship.

Touch is, of course, an integral part of many modern healing practices — for example, chiropractic, osteopathic, physiotherapy and therapeutic massage. In addition to the structural, manipulative skills shown by these practices, subtle healing bonds are also at work.

Although these professional groups are battling, often with success, to be accepted into the evidence-based world of orthodoxy, many are recognising that they also are healers. Many practices, such as craniosacral osteopathy, involve subtle exchanges of energy, more closely related to the therapeutic touch and the Chinese practice of *qi-gong* than more mechanical forms of manipulation. Hopefully, an open recognition of these issues will not be perceived as a threat to these professional groups but rather with the respect that healing practices deserve.

Cranio-sacral therapy, which involves the gentle placement of the healer's hands over the scalp, is most effective when the healer is in relaxed, open, channelling mode — a gentle altered state, acting as a receiver of information from the environment. The same applies to the masseur and acupuncturist. *Hakomi* therapy is a version of this — Hakomi is a Hopi Indian name meaning 'Who are you?' The healer sits quietly alongside the patient in a receptive mindful state, an open door to the information exchange between healer and patient, and the environment.

Acupuncture needles are, as we described in Chapter 9, 'aerials' that help transmit this information in and out of the body. As I gently touch a needle, the patient feels a sensation running through them, especially if I have found the right point on the meridian. I explain that this is precisely what happens when I try to move a portable television aerial in an attempt to get a better picture. As I hold on to the 'rabbit's ears', the picture is perfect, only to deteriorate when I move back to join my family watching impatiently from their comfortable chairs.

'Just stand there until the programme's finished, Dad,' they say. All fathers have been in this position at least once in their lives.

If the rabbit's ears are lost, then placing one's finger over the aerial-in socket usually produces some sort of picture, especially if the reception is good and the television is in reasonable working order. Likewise, therapeutic touch practices such as the one we demonstrated in Chapter 9 do not need conducting metal needles.

Enhanced healing — playing the crowd

We are seeing a picture emerging of the healer acting as a kind of surrogate between the patient and the environment. A conductor and channeller of information balanced by the wide diversity of nature. The Schumann Resonances, which result from the lightning strikes over the tropical rainforests, represent one measurement of this information.

As well, the healer can enlist help from not just the environment but from 'working an audience'.

As soon as I started to become enthusiastic about acupuncture, I attended as many seminars and demonstrations as possible. I witnessed remarkable events — armed with only a single needle, a renowned professor of acupuncture would appear to cure in an instant painful conditions that rookies such as myself were struggling to make an impression on.

Shoulders 'frozen' for months thawed in a flash before our eyes, leaving their owners delighted but baffled, often to the spontaneous applause of a traditionally reserved audience of world-weary medics.

The painful condition invariably returned over the next two days; we repeated the process in the sober surroundings of our own rooms, only to find that our results were rather less dramatic. We further repeated the ritual four or five more times, and although the pains seldom returned to their original state, the miraculous events we had witnessed at the hands of the master alluded us. We were left somewhat in awe of the wisdom, skill and secret powers of these 'acupuncture gurus'.

However, as we evolved into teachers ourselves, we noticed similar phenomena. It became clear that we could tap into the enthusiasm of a group to enhance the effects of our demonstrations. Sensations were more likely to be felt travelling along the acupuncture meridian of the students in response to inserting a needle on a distant point.

Working a crowd is an essential part of show business. The comedian bonds the audience instantly through laughter; the singer draws them together emotionally, immersing them in a communal act of focused listening. Even the driest of university lecturers tries to grab the attention of his audience with a witty comment early on in his monologue.

It is important, though, when teaching healing techniques, to make students aware of this group effect and its implications. The group members should be intricately involved, and permitted to bask in the glory as much as the 'wise' demonstrator. Once the group is properly informed and educated, that focused group energy can be used to the greater good.

Evidence of this has been shown by David Spiegel's support groups for the sufferers of breast cancer, described in Chapter 2.

Group work is now a blueprint for modern business practices, with their focus on networking rather than single personalities. Creativity is enhanced by groups in a way that exceeds the sum of its parts. Consider the Beatles, the Marx Brothers and, according to my daughters, the Spice Girls and Boyzone.

Communal healing ceremonies have the same ingredients. A congregation is guided into a state of focused togetherness, often through singing or praying. The conducting minister then may act as a channeller for a benevolent, omnipotent God.

I do not see it as my role to advocate or promote any religious belief. However, I try to encourage a free discussion of spiritual issues during a consultation, especially if the patient is actively involved in a religious or spiritual organisation. The healing ceremony can be a positive intro-duction to the process of deep healing but it can also leave someone feeling vulnerable, behoven to the organisation or individual healer. It is what follows the dramatic 'honeymoon' stage that is so critical for deep healing. It can be the difference between freedom and dependence.

Healing rituals and ceremonies are merely stepping-stones leading us to a more healthy place. A stepping-stone is no place to be left stranded.

So the *intent* behind the healing becomes critical. The outcome may even hinge on something so difficult to gauge — especially for someone who has been starved of unconditional love.

These are the questions we should ask ourselves whenever we become involved with a healing group:

1. Can I discuss these issues with someone of influence within the group?
2. Do I feel fully informed?
3. What are the financial ties to the group? How binding are they?
4. Are they listening to me?
5. Do they want to convert me to their way of thinking?
6. How involved do I feel?
7. Would I feel guilty if I left?

Ultimately it comes down to a gut feeling about the organisation — that small inner voice. I have attended many seminars expounding the virtues of a wide range of healing disciplines. At one such meeting recently, I asked a leading proponent of a certain type of meditation about his views on the teachings of another school.

'What do they know about meditation?' he bristled indignantly.

It seemed that his own techniques had failed to promote within himself a sublime state of peaceful co-existence.

My advice to all concerned is to ask precisely this type of question of their new mentors, observing them closely for signs of humility, patience and forgiveness.

Electronic freedom — avoiding control

Our friendly electron 'Blur' also yearns to work as a free agent. She exists in a vast quantum field, coming and going at her leisure until we fix her in our sites. She then settles into a precise orbit, but it is 'Blur' who decides whether this is up or down. This occurs completely randomly, so science cannot as yet predict this; and what is unpredictable remains uncontrollable.

It is known that a tight, sure bond is formed by entanglement, and that electrons find 'mates' who always spin in opposite directions to themselves. But which way they spin is a completely random event. We are made up of trillions of electrons like 'Blur', each capable of forming these bonds that transcend time and space, but the direction of each spin is in 'the lap of the gods'. An infinitely complex jumble — a code that can't be broken by logical thought. So, as yet we can't fax ourselves around as in *Star Trek*; neither, thankfully, can we create or destroy ourselves. The system carries with it remarkable in-built safety features that protect it from being tampered with by modern-day Dr Frankensteins.

It is likely, however, that we are seeing the transfer of quantum information 'in action' with the telepathic studies co-ordinated from Princeton University. Both the percipients and the agents — the human transmitters of this quantum information — seem at their most effective when they release control; when they open themselves up to each other and their environment. They then record their information, converting their experiences into ways we can interpret objectively — drawing pictures, and filling in check sheets.

Producing objective data out of such subjective experiences has proved a real problem throughout history. Healers have frequently had difficulty explaining their gifts to others in logical terms, leaving sceptics unimpressed. Grigory Rasputin, the renowned Russian monk and healer, is usually remembered as a rough, womanising, mystical figure who fell in and out of favour with the ruling Romanov family. Despite being illiterate (and by all accounts rather unkempt), he was revered by Tzar Nicholas and Alexandra, who enlisted his help because their son's haemophilia was not responding to orthodox treatment. After a while, the ruling family felt he was a bad influence on Alexandra and Russia as a whole, and plotted to dispose of him. As with many healers throughout history, he met a decidedly sticky end. Having failed to kill him with poisoned cakes and wine, his persecutors shot him several times, bound him, and eventually threw him still alive into a river.

But there was another side to Rasputin; he impressed all those who sought his help with his calm ways, listening skills, and insights into the future.[70] For all his worldly indiscretions, he was, it appears, an ideal transmitter of quantum information.

Fields

> I know that this defies the law of gravity but, you see, I never studied law.
>
> — BUGS BUNNY

Science has now progressed past the tangible and visible into studying bonds that have the potential to link all matter in the universe. Step by step, we are being led to places that mechanistic, Newtonian science with all its logic cannot take us. We are trying to understand mysterious concepts such as 'fields' of information, which are apparently immune to the laws of gravity and even our own fixed ideas of time and space. So what exactly are these fields, and what properties do they have that can help us understand more about them and their role in healing?

Holographic fields

One reason I was initially attracted to the art of acupuncture was its simplicity. I was delighted to find ways of relieving discomfort that were swift, painless and occasionally dramatic. Ear acupuncture fulfilled these criteria admirably; there was the added advantage that patients never had to remove their clothes. They could even walk around, or go back into the waiting room, with the tiny needles in their ears. Ear acupuncture honours a theory that somehow there is a whole map of our body over our external ear (see figure below).

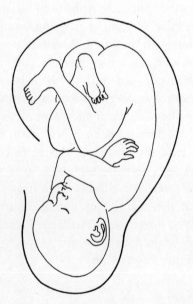

The holographic 'map' of the baby within the ear (artistic impression)

In practice, this is a remarkably effective form of treatment. A tiny needle inserted into the area corresponding to the neck can relieve pain more quickly than the time it takes to write out a prescription. A small ball-bearing or seed can be taped to the spot for continuous relief.

When I started to do this I had no idea why it worked. There seemed to be no logical scientific reason, apart from the fact that a branch of the vagus nerve reached the surface of our bodies in the ear. But this didn't explain why a needle placed three millimetres away from another needle relieved pain at a different part of the body.

The work of physicist Dennis Gabor now goes some of the way to explaining this. In 1971 he won a Nobel prize for his research into the holographic nature of fields.

We are all familiar now with holograms — those transparent though lifelike, three-dimensional models that we can walk around and view from different angles. They are produced when two beams of laser light meet, one of which has rebounded off, or photographed, a three-dimensional object, such as a flower. First, a laser beam is split into two component beams — one that rebounds off the flower, and a second that is simply reflected off a mirror. They meet up again to form an *inter-ference* pattern, similar to that observed when ripples meet from two stones dropped into a still pool.

This pattern is recorded on a photographic plate (see figure (a) below). Remarkably, when a further single laser beam is directed onto this photographic message, a three-dimensional image results; the memory of the rebounding beam has been retained[71] (see figure (b) overleaf).

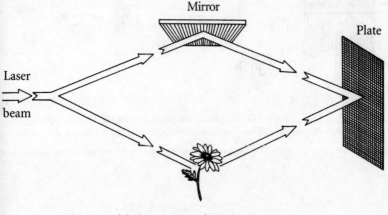

(a) The creation of a hologram

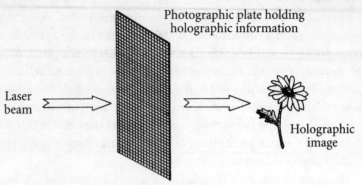

(b) The creation of a hologram

So we are beginning to understand more about information transfer within the three-dimensional world. Closer to the realities of nature.

But what Dennis Gabor discovered was even more remarkable. If a corner of the photographic plate that carried the holographic information was cut off and subjected to a beam of laser light, an exact replica of the *whole* would result. And this occurred no matter how small the piece or how many times it was done. With a hologram, every piece contains the whole! (See figure below.)

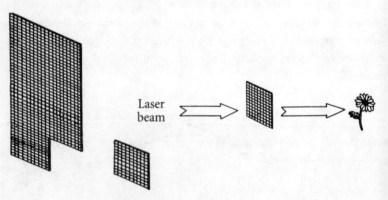

(c) An exact replica hologram produced by cutting off one corner of the photographic plate

Strange though this may seem, we do not have to look far in nature to see this pattern in action. For example, if we divide up a magnet into several smaller parts, we see that each will retain its magnetic properties.

Similarly, every one of our cells, every strand of DNA, holds enough information to build a whole duplicate body of 'us'. A Rumanian scientist, Ioan Dumitrescu, has even demonstrated this effect in a living leaf.[72] First, he cut a circular hole in the leaf, which he then subjected to an 'electrographic' scanning process. Within the hole there appeared an image of the whole leaf with a tiny hole in it!

Holographic leaf within a leaf (after Dr I. Dumitrescu)

We can also see a basis for our ear microsystem, and with it a step to validate all the other microsystems that have for years so perplexed conventional doctors.

These include:

◆ The map over the iris in the eye used by naturopaths and iridology practitioners.
◆ The map on the soles of the feet massaged by reflexologists.
◆ The map on the palm used by those who study palmistry.
◆ The map on the tongue 'read' by Chinese doctors.
◆ The wrist pulses felt and analysed by Chinese doctors.

It also lends support to the fundamental premise of holistic practices such as Chinese medicine that view the body as a 'microcosmic' mirror of the 'macrocosmic' universe.

There are also theories proposed that the holographic field of information acts like a map for our development. We can now see how an ordinance survey map of the whole body can be carried by each cell. The DNA has the know-how to produce all the right cells, or building blocks, but it is the fields that direct the DNA to the right place. It is as if we have all the pieces for our jigsaw but we need a picture to build it on. The esoteric literature equates this with our *etheric field*.

Morphogenetic fields

We have seen that the bonds of entanglement seem to know no physical boundaries. Instant connections inside and outside us, with people and things no matter what the distance. The PEAR experiments also showed that all this occurred even when machines were switched off — that such connections extended across time. The proponents of the theory of morphogenetic fields cite nature as providing further clues to our habits and our existence.

The theory of morphogenetic fields proposes that the fields of information are fundamental to our being. Not only are they in instant and constant communication with others like us now, but also others in the past. That our habits, good and bad, can be influenced by those who have gone before, stored in our vast memory bank. This also applies to ourselves. Because time is irrelevant for these links, we are in contact with the memory of our own past habits. In a way, the person we know best is our 'past self' — who we try to learn to love, warts and all. The evolutionary biologist Rupert Sheldrake proposed that many patterns of behaviour in the animal world can be explained with this model:

◆ How migrating birds 'know' when and where to travel their great distances.
◆ How whole species 'learn' specific habits simultaneously while separated by vast distances.
◆ How lost animals and birds find their way back home, even when their homes are moved.

He defines the sharing of these fields as 'morphic resonance'. As with all other living beings, we humans 'resonate' more closely with those most like us. This seems another way of explaining entanglement, but it also honours the harmonious nature of fields.[73]

Sheldrake's hypothesis of morphic resonance blends comfortably with the healer/patient model we have already explored. Here, the healer's role can be seen as having two components:

1. As a transmitter of the world's 'morphic' resonances, diffused and averaged out by nature.
2. The healer's own field resonating with that of the patient. With trust, two fields can start to resonate, blending with each other. An example of this is the master/apprentice relationship.

The apprentice 'taps' into the accumulated experience and wisdom of the master. The master's 'morphogenetic field' is in 'morphic resonance' with his or her own past: experience is handed on. Here, information from all previous healer/patient bonds can contribute to the process.

Repeated meetings can reinforce these messages, producing the 'physiological relearning' pattern I talked of previously in Chapter 9.

Although these bonds are 'non-local' and distance healing is becoming validated, the physical meeting of the two parties provides the best chance for resonance. This may reflect our current state of evolution: information from all our past meetings and all those who we resonate with are more relevant than our distant telepathic contacts.

Many spiritual healers, employing the 'laying-on of hands' or therapeutic touch, claim an awareness of field variations as their hands pass over diseased areas. Although practices vary, the healers strive to achieve resonance between their own conducting fields and those of their patients.

Morphic resonance may also shed light onto the controversial issue of 'remembering past lives' and communication through mediums with those who have died. The bonds we form with loved ones don't disappear when that person dies. Their memory is retained and stored and our friendship continues in the same way as it does with our own past. With this model, it is not an extreme view to say that, in essence, our loved ones live on within us and others.

Jung's 'collective unconscious'

These ideas parallel Carl Jung's theory of the *collective unconscious*: the subconscious coming together of like, focused minds — a joint awareness — which provides a basis for group prayer and directed meditation. This may also explain the synchronicity of creative ideas such as fashion trends, and the global expression of deeply held feelings as occurred with the outpouring of grief that followed the death of Princess Diana in 1997. The growing worldwide concern about genetic engineering is thought by many to be a reflection of this pattern of collective awareness.

Bohm's 'implicate order'

Another closely related concept is proposed by physicist Professor David Bohm of London University. He describes two levels of existence — the *explicate order* and the *implicate order*.

1. The explicate order

This is what we encounter in our day-to-day lives. We have a good day, then a bad day. Our football team wins, then loses. We have a flat tyre, we burn the vegetables, tell a new joke. The small stuff, the trivia of our day-to-day lives, for which we can often find a good cause-effect explanation. Our team lost because the referee lacked our own acute powers of observation.

2. The implicate order

This is altogether more subtle. Background trends, less logical and open to reason. The reason we revert to our old habits. Why we ask ourselves 'When will we ever learn?'

It concerns the patterns of our lives. Events that link together as if through 'fate'. The patterns that seem to become more easy to see in retrospect, with hindsight. The order that is more profound than the day-to-day ups and downs and the understanding conveyed when we say, 'Well, it just wasn't meant to be.' It concerns the deeper aspects of unconditional love that we struggle to define. Why, when and with whom we fall in love.

This whole concept is important to deep healing. We have seen that healing appears to progress haphazardly if we see only the *explicate* pattern.

We try to find reasons for this day-to-day chaos. What did I do wrong? What was it I ate? All the consequences of our conditioning in 'The Age of Reason'.

The healer's job is, through listening, to stand outside the 'trivia' of the explicate order, thereby helping the patient to identify the *implicate order* within his or her life. The 'meaning' is so often hidden there.

These insights and philosophies are, I suspect, describing similar phenomena in slightly differing ways. Common to all is an evolving awareness, or consciousness, that there are connections between all things that defy many of the laws of classical physics, which were drawn up before the dawn of the twentieth century.

Pondering these issues, Albert Einstein was to observe wryly: 'Gravity cannot be held responsible for people falling in love.'

Messages in water

For every single molecule of protein in our bodies, there are 10,000 molecules of water. We have seen how effectively water transmits vibrations of low frequencies, allowing whales to communicate with each other at vast distances. Submarines communicate using this low frequency. Hippopotami emit sounds under water that can be heard 35 kilometres up-river.

We have also seen evidence that low frequencies can be recorded within the body, with research underway to find out whether bands of connective tissue, which have the property of binding water, actually correspond to the ancient Chinese meridian lines.

The basis of homoeopathy continues to be the subject of much scepticism with its protagonists being accused of gullibility, naïvety and even greed. The sceptics despair that anyone could be so stupid as to think that diluting a chemical to the extent that there is no active compound left could leave a compound such as water with any potency at all.

Dr Jacques Benveniste is one of the world's leading researchers in the highly controversial area of *water memory*.[74] His research suggests that water acts as a very sophisticated hi-fi system, amplifying and recording the body's messages. For example, he proposes that an adrenalin molecule enlists the help of all its surrounding water molecules to get its message across. It attaches itself to its receptors, say in the heart, and starts vibrating. The surrounding water molecules vibrate too, carrying the signal just as the sea transmits messages from a submarine. He proposes that the water amplifies the message, and even stores the data (information) as memory. His current research takes this even further:

> We have recently completed very simple experiments showing that a molecule at a normally active concentration does not work in a medium devoid of water.

To make more sense of water's role as a 'medium', we should return to the open-air rock concert we first visited in Chapter 7.

The rock concert — Visualisation Part 2

The artist appears on stage with her band in front of 60,000 adoring fans, all keen to start dancing and have a good time. She starts to sing but no one can hear her. Something in the amplification system is faulty. No matter how well she sings and the band plays, no one can dance. The road crew try, under mounting pressure, to isolate and sort out the problem; they discover that the microphones themselves are the cause. It appears that they can't be fixed and there are no replacements. Our lead singer becomes impatient and storms off the stage. The management have to think quickly; the crowd is restless and booing.

They decide to play the rock star's latest album, recorded recently at a major studio. They place it into the CD player, and turn the volume up loud. The crowd start to dance, and our star, who has now recovered her poise, reappears, miming to her own recording to the cheers of her still-adoring fans.

The next day the crowd has gone, and the stage is bare. The place is a mass of litter. Scores of festival staff wade their way dejectedly through piles of rubbish, cleaning, sorting and discarding. To raise their spirits, our star's CD is played through the PA system. They respond by moving rhythmically to the beat, attending to their unenviable task with renewed vigour.

Let's draw some comparisons.

1. Amplification: Water, it is proposed, acts in the body as an 'amplifier'. The messages from active compounds such as adrenalin, and many peptides, that need to get through to the tissues need amplification. Adding water in increasing measures to a homoeopathic solution is like turning up the volume on the hi-fi.

2. Recording: Our rock star had recently recorded an album at a recording studio. Her voice was 'memorised' as data onto a compact disc. This could then be replayed, even when she had gone home — it did not need her to be present. The recording equipment could even replay her music at a greater amplification than she recorded it.

Water also, it is proposed, has the property of recording, memorising data. Once memorised, it doesn't need the active compound to be present for replay.

— just like our rock star doesn't have to be present in our living room for us to play her music.

Our rock concert has been visited by a time traveller from the eighteenth century. He is intrigued, confused and deafened. He is, after all, coming directly from an era of soothing symphonic music before the days of electronic amplification and recording. Naturally enough, he is completely taken in by the singer miming the words of her own songs. But this does not match his total bewilderment the next day when he witnesses the music repeated, word for word, bar for bar, with no singer or band in sight.

Our time traveller is understandably confused, as he has come from another era. A time when the concept of a mechanical world was gaining strength — the dawn of the industrial and technological age.

Those scientists and doctors involved in highly technical specialities today may be in a similar state of confusion by this new way of thinking. However, there is common ground. Two modern inventions have revolutionised how we receive detailed information about ourselves, and our universe, by identifying and recording the vibratory frequency of atoms — the *magnetic resonance imaging (MRI)* scanner, and the *radiotelescope*. These advances in modern physics seem to pose less of a threat to mainstream medicine than Jacques Benveniste's theories of water memory. To the passive observer, the gap between biomedicine and holistic science appears to be closing rapidly.

It will be intriguing to see whether research in the twenty-first century will confirm water as playing a vital role in transmitting, storing and organising information within the body — information received internally through the bodymind network, and externally from the environment.

It will also be interesting to see whether this leads to new ways of treating many medical conditions such as chronic illness and allergies that continue to defy modern conventional medicine.

Muscle testing — questions and answers

One testing method widely used by complementary practitioners has a variety of labels including muscle testing and *kinesiology*. There are many variations of this technique, but I will try to convey the principles and essence of the procedure here rather than the details.

The therapist tests the patient's strength using a particular set of muscles. She may ask him to make an O-ring between his thumb and one of his fingers, which she will try to prise open. Alternatively, she may ask him to raise his straightened arm away from his body, as she tries to resist his movement (see figure below).

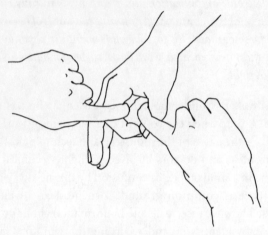

O-Ring muscle testing (other fingers may be used)

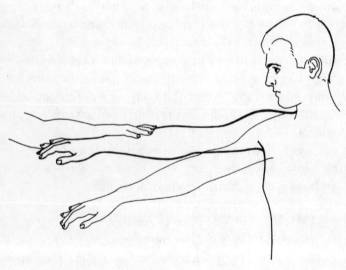

Muscle testing — shoulder

A question (information) is then posed to the patient's body by:

a. Asking the patient to hold a suspected 'toxin' in his hand. Alternatively it can be placed next to the skin. This may be a food substance, like peanuts, which is suspected to be the cause of an allergic reaction (see figure below).

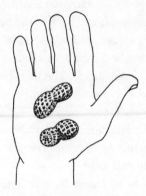

Position test object close to skin (or hold in hand) prior to muscle testing

b. The muscle testing is then repeated with a similar force of resistance. If the muscle group is now weak, it may be deduced that the substance presented is toxic to the body.

c. The patient is then asked to hold a homoeopathic remedy together with the substance. If the remedy is the correct match, the muscles will be stronger and the resistance greater (see figure below).

Retest with 'neutralising' homoeopathic remedy

With this technique, a healer/patient bond is important. A non-controlling relationship will lessen the chance of bias in the testing. And as we have seen earlier in this chapter, entangled healer/patient bonds may actually promote the transmission of information from the substance to the patient. This 'quantum' information can then be translated into binary information — muscle is either strong or it isn't.

This is similar to what occurs at a good 'listening session'. The listener repeats the words she has just heard back to the person to confirm she is truly listening. And the person, in turn, responds 'yes' or 'no'.

As well, there can often be a subtle interaction of 'fields' between the therapist, patient and the substance. The therapist may simply use the healer/patient bond, verbally questioning the patient's body while testing the muscle.

Other therapists use a machine — a black box or a computer. In this scenario, we now have therapist/patient/substance/machine all interacting and bonding with each other.

If a child or baby is to be tested, a parent may be asked to act as a surrogate, and so the links or bonds are further extended.

I am often asked about these procedures since patients are often left confused, not knowing whether to trust the findings of the practitioner. I advise them to ask themselves how they felt about the practitioner — their gut feeling. The intent of the healer is important. It should be open, unassuming, confident, and never overpowering or controlling. The patient should feel at ease with the situation.

The theories presented in this chapter, although not validating muscle testing, at least provide us with a framework through which it can be examined scientifically. However, its investigation must be handled delicately and with open minds. The bonds formed between the main players in this scene are subtle. Nearly a century ago, Albert Einstein drew the scientific world's attention to the important role of the observer — one implication of his general theory of relativity. A controlling, biased observer's field may well interact with subtle healing bonds, adversely affecting the outcome.

I have also long been aware of how important the patient's state of mind is to the outcome. A relaxed, confident outlook is as important for the patient as it is to the healer. Indeed, one can lead to another in a state of 'coherence' or resonance.

Even if a healer/patient bond has been established, a negative or angry presence in the room — a critical relative for instance — seems to block any satisfactory treatment. Although this phenomenon is anecdotal, every healing practitioner I have discussed this with is aware of these effects. As yet we do not have the scientific answers to this. Does it result from either the patient or healer being anxious? Is there direct interference from this third party to the resonance of the healer/patient bond?

One researcher, Dr Anna Rolfes, has attempted to investigate whether negative emotions do indeed affect muscle testing.[75] A medical doctor trained in orthopaedic surgery and osteopathy, Anna now works as a kinesiologist in Australia. She asked students who said they feared failing their exams to imagine that this had actually happened. Those who had other fears had to pretend living through their own 'anxiety scene'. These groups were compared with a control group who imagined being 'gently massaged'.

The results were inconclusive. They do, however, form a starting point for further research into this complex area.

Systems theory

> Like a circle in a spiral, like a wheel within a wheel,
> Never ending or beginning on an ever spinning reel
> As the images unwind, like the circles that you find
> in the windmills of your mind.
> — MARILYN AND ALAN BERGMAN, 'The Windmills of Your Mind'

We are becoming aware of our bodies not as isolated closed systems, but as integrated *open systems*. Systems theory is concerned more with the relationships between objects than the objects themselves. For the systems thinker, the relationships are primary.

The metaphors, quotes and poems I have used in this book can be viewed simply as tools for familiarising and illustrating new and strange concepts; systems thinkers, however, may take this a step further. They will be at pains to point out the holographic nature of the universe, the ever-repeating patterns, the wheels within wheels. Rather than suggesting that what happened at our open-air rock concert was merely similar to the ways emotions influence our bodies, they will declare that they are precisely the same. Emotions *are* the music of the body.

To the systems thinker, illnesses not only reflect the internal workings of our bodies but the state of the environment in which we live. If our resistance is low — if we are 'thin-skinned' — we will absorb the problems of the world like a sponge. Many of the chronic conditions that plague us in the modern world — depression, chronic fatigue syndrome, occupational overuse — can be seen to mirror what is happening around us in the world. And yet the focus of research is so often to identify the chemical changes within the body, so that another chemical — a pain-killing drug or an anti-depressant — can be added to 'correct' the problem. This approach is undoubtedly effective in many cases and offers valuable relief from symptoms, but it has tremendous limitations.

It largely ignores society's role and responsibilities. A convenient answer is provided in the form of a pill, developed by people with specialised expertise in a manner most 'lay' people don't understand. The patient, or sufferer, does not become involved. The Chinese understand this, and it is best expressed in their proverb:

> Tell me and I'll forget; show me and I may remember; involve me and I'll understand.

Unfortunately, the bio-medical paradigm has not yet embraced many of the concepts presented in this book. The range of sensitivity of our bodies, which appears so vital to the development of these evolving conditions, is a subject orthodox medicine has largely neglected. The diehard proponents of orthodox, conventional medicine are not systems thinkers.

The Gaia hypothesis

In Greek mythology Gaia was the Earth Goddess. She gave birth to Uranos, the male Sky-God 'so he might surround her and cover her completely and be a secure home for the blessed gods forever'.[76]

Gaia was re-introduced to the modern world by NASA scientist and environmentalist James Lovelock in 1982 with his proposal that the earth was alive.[77] He redefined the earth itself as a living system, of which we humans were a part. If we were capable of viewing earth from a distance, as lunar astronauts, we would see a dynamic, apparently living object. Changing colours, clouds continually moving and reforming. Like the ancient Chinese, we would see all elements of the earth interacting and supporting each other. If it were possible to watch for millions of years, we would see that the land masses, the countries and continents were not static, but continuously drifting, redefining their borders. We would begin to ponder our role in this giant, living organism. It is as if each person contributes and relates to the earth in the way a single cell relates to our own body.

This unique vision of the world has helped to spawn a deeper understanding of ecology — now popularly known as *deep ecology*. Environmental issues are not regarded as important solely for the survival of mankind; the world is not there simply for us. Rather we humans are seen as an integral part of the system, inter-relating and ideally nurturing Mother Earth, treating her with the respect we pay our own mothers. Giving and receiving with the right intent.

Deep ecologists are concerned about the whole system, of which we are one vital part. If we exert control over the environment for our own selfish motives, will it be able to support and nurture all of nature in the same way?

Under systems theory, illnesses such as depression and chronic fatigue states can be viewed as 'bulletin boards' on the current state of Gaia. Because sufferers are sensitive, they absorb the ills of the world in the way canaries absorbed the toxic gas methane in a coal mine. In the same way that a canary's death was evidence of the presence of methane in a mine, so too are these modern-day diseases symptomatic of a wider malaise.

Love and the healing intent

I may not be a smart man but I know what love is.
— FORREST GUMP

The first duty of love is to listen.
— PAUL TILLICH, GERMAN EXISTENTIALIST PHILOSOPHER

For something so essential to our survival, modern medicine has surprisingly little to say about love. Maybe there are good reasons for not analysing love too closely. No sooner have we studied and measured something than we start to want to control it. We set up guidelines, protocols and conditions for its use. For the moment then, perhaps it is better for love to remain mysterious and unconditional.

But loving intent is essential to healing. The landmark studies we have explored are studies of 'aspects of love' — from David Spiegel's breast cancer support groups to delays in wound healing evident when one cares for a loved one with Alzheimer's disease. Even the human/machine interactions work better when a 'love-bond' is established with the machine. And my golf definitely improves when I use my beloved putter.

Healing can only proceed in an environment of love. Naturally, this doesn't mean healers 'fall in love' with their patients but it does mean that common bonds have to be established. Trusting non-judgemental friendships in an atmosphere of honesty and kindness.

Healers should be prepared for these bonds to be tested by their patients, especially those who have been let down by previous relationships. They may look for the catch, the condition, sometimes quickly finding your Achilles heel, your sore point. They may arrive late for an appointment, not pay fees, or criticise a personal friend.

I have witnessed the most remarkable breakthroughs in healing result from the most difficult of challenges. The healer can react to these situations honestly, even revealing his own anger and hurt. An honest expression of emotions. But an air of forgiveness should prevail (on both sides), and I suspect this forms the basis of a trusting friendship.

The healing value of friendship cannot be overstated. We have already described this in terms of morphic resonance but the words of author Anaïs Nin evoke an even more poignant image of true friendship:

> Each friend represents a world in us, a world possibly not born until they arrive, and it is only in meeting them a new world is born.

Not only should each healer become a friend, each friend becomes a healer. Just how we should behave is found not in the pages of medical journals but in the literature of the world's religions. A golden rule common to all is to treat others in the way we like to be treated ourselves:

> *Islam*: 'No one of you is a believer until he loves for his brother what he loves for himself.'

> *Taoism*: 'Regard your neighbour's gain as your gain, and your neighbour's loss as your loss.'

> *Hinduism*: 'That is the sum of duty; do naught to others which if done to thee would cause thee pain.'

> *Confucianism*: 'Is there any one maxim which ought to be acted upon throughout one's life? Surely the maxim of loving-kindness is such. Do not do unto others what you would not they should do unto you.'

> *Buddhism*: 'Hurt not others with that which pains yourself.'

> *Christianity*: 'All things whatsoever you would that men should do unto you, do ye even so to them, for this is the law and the prophets.'

Of all the healers throughout history, Jesus of Nazareth has been the most closely studied. Reports of his healing acts provide us with many insights, especially through his humility and forgiveness. The love he proposed was 'patient and kind'. He stressed the importance of faith and hope — two essential ingredients of healing. To this list he added 'love'.

'But the greatest of these is love.'

— 1 CORINTHIANS 13:13

Healing touch

The world today is hungry not only for bread but hungry for love; hungry to be wanted, to be loved.

— MOTHER TERESA

Each of us uses touch every day to heal. Holding our loved one's hand, stroking the cat, patting the dog. Watch the contentment and compassion with which a grandmother knits a hat and booties for her newly arrived grandchild; how keen a grandfather is to mend that broken toy truck, then ruffle his grandson's hair as he proudly hands it back to him 'as good as new'.

Over the past 25 years, over 50,000 nurses have trained in the art of Therapeutic Touch (TT). This was pioneered by Dolores Krieger RN, PhD, in 1975, and follows the principles of healing I have already outlined. The practitioner is focused and relaxed, mindful of a caring and compassionate bond with the patient. The healers 'centre' them-selves, passing their hands over the patient, resting over areas of the body where there are either symptoms or 'energy blockages'. They may or may not touch the patient — some schools encourage holding the hand 7–10 centimetres above the affected area.

There are many variations of this technique, with many different labels — *qi gong*, *reiki*, laying-on of hands, intentional healing — but they all have the same principles in common:

◆ The loving intent to heal;
◆ The willingness of the healee to be healed;
◆ Acknowledging the healer as a transmitter of 'universal' energy.

Clinical trials have been encouraging, although only small studies have been performed. Pain and anxiety levels have been shown to be reduced in several patient groups receiving TT — in particular, those with arthritis of the knee,[78] and burn sufferers.[79]

Children with HIV infection have also been shown to become more relaxed in a small study at Rutgers University, USA.[80] Objective scientific evidence is emerging that the body's physiology — temperature, heart rate and muscle activity — can be influenced by 'non-contact' Therapeutic Touch.[81] Therapeutic Touch is now practised in many Western hospitals worldwide with the acceptance of a growing number of patients and health professionals including doctors.

However, not everyone is happy with this situation. The 11-year-old daughter of a known sceptic became the youngest person to have a research paper published by a leading medical journal, with her 1 April 1998 study 'disproving' Therapeutic Touch. This started out as a sixth-grade school science project but within a few weeks had been accepted by the *Journal of the American Medical Association (JAMA)*.[82] Twenty-one TT practitioners, all female, were asked to place both hands through a screen with their palms facing upwards. The young girl, Emily Rosa, hidden from view, then placed her own hand seven centimetres above one of the healer's hands. The healer then had to guess which of their hands she was above. Their guesses were no better than one would expect by chance.

The paper received massive media coverage. Emily made guest appearances on *CBS This Morning, The Today Show*, CNN, and ABC. The study received front page coverage in many US national papers, with Emily being hailed as 'the youngest person ever to publish in the prestigious *Journal of the American Medical Association*.'

To the authors, the paper represented 'proof' that the basis of TT was groundless. The editor-in-chief of *JAMA*, Dr George D. Lundberg, agreed, commenting:

> This simple statistically valid study tests the theoretical basis for 'Therapeutic Touch': the 'human energy field'. This study found that such a field does not exist.

It appears that this single project provided Dr Lundberg with sufficient evidence to disprove TT entirely. In reply to a nurse's concern that the trial was poorly designed, and had made no reference to the necessity for compassionate intent, one of the authors, Larry Sarner, concluded:

> Chasing will-o'-the-wisps like TT, by wasting professional time and holding out false hope, can reasonably be considered cruel and inhumane.[83]

I have little doubt that the authors of this study, which carries a heavy bias, represent a minority opinion. My own correspondence with them reveals that they were unaware of the recent work on 'entanglement', and that they did not refer to any modern physics because they felt it was irrelevant. They were concerned that taxpayers' money should no longer be wasted on TT, and they continue to lobby hospitals worldwide in an attempt to wipe out the practice.

Despite our more enlightened times, it seems that the path of the modern healers is no easier than their predecessors throughout history. The wise words of Mother Teresa of Calcutta provide comfort and perspective to healers whose intentions and skill are so misunderstood:

> If you do good, people may accuse you of selfish motives; do good anyway.

Creativity

Creativity is more important than knowledge.
— ALBERT EINSTEIN

When I ask a patient I am seeing for the first time about their creativity, I am surprised how often the answer is: 'Oh, I'm not really creative, you know. My sister, she's the creative one . . . oh, and my son . . . he's brilliant . . . plays the saxophone by ear . . .'

At this point, I may interrupt (politely, of course): 'So your son is creative and you are not. Let me understand this. You gave birth to this creative being, and yet you are not creative yourself?'

By definition all living creatures are creative. It is our natural state. Every thought, every sentence is a creative act. We don't have to paint like Renoir or play the saxophone like John Coltrane. Everyone has creative talents — it is simply a matter of tuning in to them. We shouldn't judge ourselves harshly or compare ourselves unfavourably with others.

Procreation and parenthood are creative states. When we reach our middle years, our creative focus may change. It may be the time we can start to see our creativity flourish. For women, this is both important and difficult. They may feel guilty about indulging in their passions — receiving joy and satisfaction in their own right. But creativity is a 'giving' act. Creating a thing of beauty, writing a poem, tending a garden can be seen as a gift to the world.

Many people involved in the creative process are aware of ideas flowing through them. A sensation of channelling ideas from 'somewhere out there'. Admittedly, the craft has to be learned — the perspiration behind the inspiration. But this eventually leads to a state of confidence and relaxation allowing the creative forces to flow.

Knowing that creativity is our natural state should free us into pursuing our dreams and passions. And whatever these are is not for others to judge. It is perfectly all right to be a passionate bank manager. The most important scientists in history have been passionate and creative people, lateral thinkers who were prone to leaping out of their baths, yelling 'Eureka'.

In our creative state there is little room for repressed feelings. We have the receiving/giving ratio in balance. We are, in turn, creating the ideal environment for healing. Could those symptoms we can't suppress — the insomnia, palpitations, restlessness — be our bodymind's way of letting us know we should be following our dreams?

Tony's story

Tony was 28 and had returned to New Zealand to 'settle down'. He had spent three years travelling around the world. The past year had seen him skippering yachts around the Caribbean and Greek Islands. He came home, feeling it was about time he 'got a proper job'.

He was a qualified electrical engineer and yearned to marry these skills with his passion for the sea. He could see himself designing, selling and demonstrating state-of-the-art navigation equipment for ocean-going yachts. The job he landed was a salesman for a mobile phone company.

To begin with he put up with the uneasy feeling 'in his guts', the palpitations, the sleeplessness. It was understandable — getting back to the real world needed some adjustment. He became depressed and was prescribed anti-depressants. Still no better. He looked around; the others in the office did not seem to be suffering. True, they did not seem passionate about the work but it wasn't making them ill.

Tony began to suffer from pains in his arms after only a few moments on his work computer. More drugs that didn't work. He had to stop work, leaving him with no money, back living with his parents.

He came to me for acupuncture which he 'really couldn't afford'. What we did was talk.

Tony's body had had a taste of the good life. It was not impressed with the current state of affairs. It seemed to be forcing him to focus on his creative needs. Sure, it wasn't logical. It didn't understand mortgages or interest rates. But, we decided, it was showing no signs of giving up on its quest.

We discussed deep healing — not simply the suppression of symptoms. We talked of the patterns in our lives, David Bohm's 'implicate order' and the Eastern concept of Dharma — the reason why we are here, our uniqueness.

I only saw Tony the one time. I wonder how he is getting on.

Health consciousness

Let us not look back in anger, not forward in fear, but around in awareness.
— JAMES THURBER

There are many ways of perceiving 'reality'. Our eyes receive light, but light occupies only one tiny band of frequencies in the whole electromagnetic spectrum. If we rely solely on our sight, we are like television sets tuned to one channel only. And this applies to all our senses — it is tempting to live in a 'fool's paradise' where the only reality is the one formed and conditioned by our five senses.

This is why deeper levels of consciousness are so often triggered following so-called *altered states*. I have noticed many who while experiencing acupuncture for the first time become aware of another dimension of their selves. They may begin to feel more intuitive or have their intuitions validated. Kinesiologists, or muscle-testing practitioners, report the sense of wonder in their clients as they observe the linking of body and mind. Near-death experiences can change someone's perception of reality forever.

One would think that medical doctors, with their scientific training, would be more convinced about acupuncture from all the evidence now to be found in the medical journals and textbooks. However, over my years of teaching acupuncture to doctors, it is the experience of the changes they feel themselves in response to a single tiny needle in their foot that really 'hooks' them in.

I have also noticed that many hanging on to a purely materialistic world view — whose lives are focused mainly on issues of control, power and conflict — remain unconvinced of the existence of a world beyond their senses (and control). No reasoned argument, no scientific advance seems to be able to jolt them out of this fixed mindset.

I have learned this lesson over the years running teaching courses for doctors and health professionals on many of the topics found in this book. I no longer try to convince others, doctors in particular, of the benefits of holistic healing; this is a journey they can only make of their own free will, when they are ready.

But our consciousness evolves not solely from our own personal experiences. The scientific advances outlined in this book, pioneered by those who combine rigour with vision, have challenged the twentieth century's most critical and brilliant minds. Chapters devoted to acupuncture are appearing in orthodox medical textbooks. Telepathy is discussed in psychology books. The boundaries between conventional and 'alternative' medicine, psychology and 'para-psychology' are blurring, and the reason is the quality of the research.

Shortly before his death in 1996, the astronomer Carl Sagan wrote a scholarly book supporting the scientific method and healthy scepticism.[84] He was, throughout his career, highly critical of the 'New Age' movement and 'pseudo-scientific' explanations of the many unproven phenomena.

But despite this, he felt that certain areas of research into extra-sensory perception deserved serious study. These included the human/machine interactions as researched by the PEAR group, and the receiving of thoughts projected at people under 'mild sensory deprivation'. Furthermore, Sagan was impressed by the scientific investigation of children recalling details of 'previous lives'. He observed that these children's accounts had been proved to be accurate through valid scientific method, with *reincarnation* being considered as a possible explanation.

One researcher who is continuing to study this phenomenon is Professor Ian Stevenson, a psychiatrist at the University of Virginia, who has examined 2500 such cases of children 'remembering' past lives. He has studied 225 children in detail, cross-checking their stories with medical and police records of deceased people. Included in his research are details of children with birthmarks that 'correspond' to lethal penetration injuries suffered by deceased persons.[85]

The scientific method often starts with a sensible but unproven hypothesis, which is first tested under rigorous laboratory conditions before being applied to the realities of the world outside. For mainstream science to accept something as fact, a theory that has reached this stage of 'proof' has to be subjected to more studies, often from a variety of of 'proof' has to be subjected to more studies, often from a variety of different scientists.

The advances I have described in this book show a remarkable consistency. Although some may be considered speculative jumps — i.e., applying entanglement theories to human interactions — the implications they carry for our future health and healing are considerable. It is interesting to note that the 'old' dualist model of the mind being located solely in our brain has never been put to such strict scientific scrutiny, yet remains accepted still by many mainstream doctors and scientists.

Most of the people I see in my practice come to me because modern biomedicine has not provided them with relief. They have chronic conditions, chronic because we have not been able to help. Only rarely do they wish to turn their back on modern medicine; their view, and my own, is that modern medicine has reached dazzling and sophisticated heights, with levels of professional skill and dedication that continue to impress all who seek its help. However, for those it has failed, we, as doctors, should ask ourselves whether the 'mechanical' model is appropriate.

Do answers lie within a broader vision of humanity, gleaned from history, literature, different cultures and, yes, modern science?

For those who continue to suffer day in day out, there is a wealth of such wisdom that can be applied. It is wrong for us to expect them to wait until 'all is proven'. Since Thomas Edison's time, we have solved a great many mysteries that are now accepted as scientific fact. But even now, as a new millennium begins, I suspect science has still unravelled little more than a 'millionth of one percent of anything'.

11. Healing in the twenty-first century

Medical technology will not answer all our health problems. It will, I am sure, do much that is wonderful. Keyhole surgery and designer drugs will continue to help us to 'get a life' — we will recover more quickly from medical and surgical procedures and have fewer side effects. The cautious use of molecular engineering techniques, will, with the right intent, ease suffering, and save lives.

But for many this will not be enough. For these people, healing answers will not be found in chemical laboratories or operating theatres. More likely, these answers will be found in society, in loving relationships, in their own past and hopefully in their future. They will be helped by health professionals who understand their own roles, their strengths and their limitations; who match their skills with compassion, their knowledge with humility. Professionals who take the time to guide and listen before prescribing or operating, professionals who allow patients the freedom to heal.

So this is my wish list for the century ahead. An era in which we should all play a part, taking responsibility for our own healing, and for the healing of others.

1. The internet revolution
Loneliness is the enemy of chronic illness. Support groups have flourished in the last 10 years, and are becoming increasingly sophisticated. They are now evolving into centres of learning, information and healing with the control firmly in the hands of the sufferers.

The internet and other wonders of the information age will unite the sufferers of rare and chronic illnesses from all corners of the globe. Information will be sought and analysed by group members, whose expertise will grow and flourish. Experts from all health fields will be invited to help and advise, and possibly even be employed by these groups. They will attract sponsors who will help fund research into areas of their healing previously neglected.

Multinational communication and computer companies will see the human body as a complex and wonderful quantum information storage system, and fund research into this emerging 'paradigm' for mutual benefit.

2. Global awareness

A deeper understanding of 'where we fit' in the world will develop. The Gaia hypothesis will become mainstream, with a growing respect for our harmony with nature. We will relate to the earth as we do to ourselves and our loved ones. The healing powers of nature will be rediscovered, using ancient knowledge and modern science.

As the developed countries become more globally aware, there will be less individual reliance on pharmaceuticals. As a result there will be:

◆ Less drug prescribing.
◆ Less side effects; at present serious side effects of drugs account for 6–10 percent of all hospital admissions.[86]
◆ Less antibiotic-resistant strains of bacteria. The death rate from 'multi-drug resistant tuberculosis' is now 70 percent in the USA.[87]
◆ Less money spent on drugs.

In 1990 the US spent $37.7 billion on prescriptions. By 1997 that had risen to $78.9 billion.[88]

According to the Centers for Disease Control and Prevention, Atlanta, of the 150 million prescriptions written per year for antibiotics in the USA, one-third are unnecessary.

Savings made will be redirected to global health concerns. At present a third of the world — two billion people — are infected with tuberculosis.[87] Money saved will be pooled to improve nutrition and living conditions, the underlying causes of ill health.

3. Paying in kind

Healing awareness and research will lead to a greater understanding of the role of compassionate intent. Communities will assume responsibility for the health of their members. People will take direct action. Rather than taxpayer funds going to bureaucratic agencies, people will use their spare time as volunteers, 'paying in kind'.

With advancing communication technology, the community will become truly global. Money donated to developing countries will be better used, not lost to agencies. There will be less need to genetically engineer crops to feed the world, as organically grown food and resources will be better distributed. People will realise that charity begins at home, and that small compassionate thoughts and deeds are valuable contributors to the 'compassion epidemic'.

Focused prayer and community activities will be seen as valid, 'evidence-based' ways to help all sorts of health and community issues. Laughter, creativity and joy will be truly valued as healing tools.

Everyone will realise her or his own healing potential.

4. New medicine

At present over 50 medical schools in the US offer undergraduates courses in spirituality in medicine. This will grow to become the normal practice in all medical schools.

Biophysics, energetic and information medicine will be further researched. We will recognise that the old method of testing — double-blind controlled trials — is often inadequate and too unsophisticated to measure the effects of this new medicine.

The placebo effect will be defined and understood. The effects of the observer will be taken into account. Scientists and healers will develop more appropriate ways to evaluate healing methods.

Doctors will be encouraged to study the humanities, including literature.

5. Healing and curing — side by side

Biomedicine, with its complex curing procedures that require high levels of skill, will continue to evolve. Highly skilled specialists will work alongside holistic health professionals.

The progress in genetic engineering will be balanced by our awareness of the importance of 'fields', which will place our knowledge about the structure of genes in true proportion.

The importance of 'intent' will spread even to those in the biomedical specialties. Healing touch will be understood, and integrated into mainstream care.

Eastern medicine will be studied with the new scientific methods. Eastern and Western medicine will become outdated terms as a new 'world' medicine evolves. Religious philosophies will blend in a similar way.

6. Listening
All medical and surgical interventions will be preceded by *real* listening.

7. Messages for the future
Symptoms and new illnesses will be analysed in a broader light as reporting the warning signs of society's disharmony. Holistic causes will be sought and appreciated alongside state-of-the-art diagnostic scanners.

Evolutionary trends will be appreciated with the need to accept and treat each new generation in their own terms, in their own right. Their sensitivities and their cultural heritage will be honoured.

> I have spread my dreams under your feet,
> Tread softly, because you tread on my dreams.
>
> — W. B. YEATS

Generosity of spirit

Healing is our birthright, a natural state that we all deserve. We are all healers, we are all responsible. Freeing ourselves from worry, fear and guilt also frees us to heal others. There is no such thing as an insignificant healing act. Each act of kindness — to ourselves, to others, to nature — has the real potential of flowing on, spreading its message far and wide.

Loving, forgiving relationships can overcome suffering and disease — such words have always been comforting and inspirational. Now, however, they are also becoming scientific. A softer science but no less powerful. A necessary counterbalance to the technology of biomedicine — the *yin* to its *yang*.

Twenty years ago, it would have been difficult for a doctor to write a book on healing. In those days many health professionals felt the future lay solely in the chemical and surgical correction of deficits detected by increasingly sophisticated and accurate diagnostic machines. Medicine was becoming efficient but somehow less personal, colder. The public started to explore natural and 'alternative' health in an attempt to maintain control and an understanding of their bodies. They were also seeking true caring and compassion, instinctively knowing that this was a vital ingredient missing from their prescriptions. Quite simply they were seeking ways to heal.

This is a book born not of frustration, but hope. Out of observation, instinct and wonder. If it comforts, it is because it unveils truths you have always known.

Postscript

The limpet on the ramp

There is great skill in dislodging a limpet. As a six-year-old on my first of many annual family holidays in Portstewart, Northern Ireland, I was a mere novice. I would hack away at the unfortunate mollusc with my metal spade, my red sandcastle spade.

If the first jab was inaccurate, the limpet would smartly attach itself to the rock with a mighty force. The next blow, even if on target, would do little to shift it. A third strike, by now fuelled with the fiery temper of a small boy not getting his way, would either miss altogether or crunch into the shell, obliterating the creature's home, causing messy and mortal injury in the process.

The purpose of the exercise was to collect fish bait. The limpet had a particularly succulent brown juicy part — we called it the guts — that fish viewed as a dining delicacy. It had to be attached to the hook with great skill, and further secured using fine catgut from my father's surgery. My brother would be searching for limpets with me, collecting them in his own bucket — yellow as I remember. Mine was definitely red.

At the end of the session we would compare buckets. Crunched, mangled limpets were valued less than those in pristine condition, a point not lost on my older and wiser sibling. I frequently suffered the humiliation of displaying my specimens to 'the master' in a way all those with older brothers will instantly identify with. But I was young still, I reassured myself. Plenty of time to improve on my technique.

213

My optimism was to prove justified. It was a simple matter of timing. I was to perfect the same method I used as inside-right goal striker in soccer in precisely the style of my comic hero, Roy of the Rovers.

My foot would accelerate perfectly towards the unsuspecting shellfish, striking the side of it with the toe of my white gym-shoe one millimetre above its attachment. I decelerated just in time to prevent it hurtling out of sight. At the same time I visualised that I had scored yet another goal for England in front of a frenetic and adoring crowd at Wembley Stadium.

I was to adopt this very technique when I started to play both golf and hockey — attempting to swing my club, or stick, with the same degree of skilled precision. In fact, in an ironic twist, I now visualise a golf ball lodged awkwardly in a bunker as a juicy limpet from my youth.

At the end of our road there is a concrete ramp leading down to the beach. It spends half of its existence submerged beneath the tide, which on receding leaves the occasional limpet behind to 'graze'. I was there the other day, pondering over the issues that face us in the coming century. How realistic was it to expect our conditioned world to change? Was this simply asking too much? At the same time, another part of me was, almost subconsciously, preoccupied with lining up one such limpet 'in my sights'. Before I knew it, I had executed a perfect limpet-dislodging manoeuvre, striking it deftly with the toe of my brogue. No mark was left on the shell, which skidded up the slope at a slight angle, off the ramp, eventually dropping down a narrow crevice between two rocks.

I admit to feeling quite a sense of achievement. I hadn't lost my touch after at least 35 years.

I peered down into the dark crevice, just managing to see it lying, wedged awkwardly, in a narrow gap. I reached down and, securing it between two outstretched fingers, eased it upwards, thereby lifting it free.

I was relieved to find that there was no sign of injury. I apologised quietly to it for the disturbance — the beach was thankfully deserted — and placed it on a level portion of the adjacent rock.

I remembered from my reading that limpets were not only 'grazers' but possessed remarkable powers of navigation. Probably 'resonated' morphogenetically with all the other limpets past and present, I mused.

Satisfied that all was now well, I bade it a fond farewell and proceeded up the ramp. After only a few steps, something made me hesitate, then turn back. I found the limpet, not surprisingly, just where I had left it. It had not yet had a chance to attach itself to its new neighbourhood. Maybe it was still in shock.

I picked it up and went searching for its old attachment site. Thankfully, it was still there, a faint shadow on the rough concrete. I placed the shell meticulously in position, as if it were the very last piece of a favourite jigsaw. I made my way home, contented, and rather relieved.

I returned to the ramp the following day.

The limpet, and its mark, had gone.

References

1. My story

1. Beecher, H., 'The powerful placebo', *Journal of the American Medical Association (JAMA)*, 1955, 159: 1602–6.
2. Frank, J., 'Psychotherapy of bodily illness: an overview', *Psychotherapy and Psychosomatics*, 1975, 26: 192–202.
3. Spiegel, D., et al., 'Effect of psychosocial treatment on survival of patients with metastatic breast cancer', *The Lancet*, 1989, 2(8668): 888–91.
4. Lawlis, G., 'Story-telling as therapy; implications for medicine', *Altern. Ther. Health and Med.*, 1995, 1(2): 40–5.

2. Clearing the way

5. Pert, C., Ruff, M., et al., 'Neuropeptides and their receptors: A psychosomatic network', *The Journal of Immunology*, 1985, 135(2).
6. Petrie, K., Booth, R., Pennebaker, J., et al., 'Disclosure of trauma and immune response to a hepatitis B vaccination program', *Journal of Consulting and Clinical Psychology*, 1995, 63(5): 787–92.
7. Smyth, J., Stone, A., et al., 'Effects of writing about stressful experiences on symptom reduction in patients with asthma or rheumatoid arthritis. A randomised trial', *JAMA*, 1999, 281:1304–1309.
8. Rinpoche, S., *The Tibetan Book of Living and Dying*, 1994, Rider Books, p. 202.
9. Cohen, S., Doyle, W., et al., 'Social ties and susceptibility to the common cold', *JAMA*, 1997, 277(24): 1940–4.
10. Peck, M.S., *In Search of Stones*, Simon & Schuster, 1996.
11. Kiecolt-Glaser, J., Marucha, P., et al., 'Slowing of wound healing by psychological stress', *The Lancet*, 1995, 346(8948): 1194–6.
12. Futterman, A., Kemeny, M., et al., 'Immunological variability associated with experimentally-induced positive and negative affective states', *Psychological Medicine*, 1992, 22(1): 231–38.
13. Goodwin, J., Hunt, W., Key, C., and Samet, J., 'The effect of marital status on stage, treatment, and survival of cancer patients', *JAMA*, 1987, 258(21): 3125–30.
14. Maunsell, E., Brisson, J., and Deschenes, L., 'Social support and survival among women with breast cancer', *Cancer*, 1995, 76(4): 631–7.
15. Fawzy, F., Fawzy, N., Hyun, C., et al., 'Malignant melanoma. Effects of an early structured psychiatric intervention, coping and affective state on recurrence and survival 6 years later', *Archives of General Psychiatry*, 1993, 50(9): 681–9.

4. Healing bonds

16. Benson, H. and McCallie, D., 'Angina pectoris and the placebo effect', *New England Journal of Medicine (NEJM)*, 1979, 300: 1424–9.
17. McWhinney, I., lecture given to The Art and Science of Healing Conference, Tzu Chi Institute, Vancouver, BC, Canada, Nov. 16–18 1998.
18. Jahn, R., 'Information, consciousness, and health. Report on 16 years of research', *Altern. Ther. Health and Med.*, 1996, 2(3): 32–8.
19. Bliss, J., McSherry, E., and Fassett, J., 'Chaplain intervention reduces costs in major DRGs: An experimental study', in Heffernan, H., McSherry, E., and Fitzgerald, R. (eds.), *Proceedings NIH Clinical Center Conference on*

Spirituality and Health Care Outcomes, 21 March 1995.

20. Byrd, R., 'Positive therapeutic effects of intercessory prayer in a coronary care unit population', *South Med. Journal*, 1998, 81(7): 826–9.

21. Dossey, L., *Space, Time and Medicine*, Shambala Publications, 1982.
Dossey, L., *Healing Words: The Power of Prayer and the Practice of Medicine*, Harper San Francisco, 1995.
Dossey, L., *Reinventing Medicine – Beyond mind/body to a new era in healing*, HarperCollins, 1999.

5. Healing and dying

22. Morse, M. and Perry, P., 'Transformed by the light – the powerful effect of near death experiences on people's lives', Mass Market Paperbacks, 1994.
Ring, K., *Lessons from the Light: What We Can Learn from Near-Death Experiences*, Insight Books, 1998.
Sutherland, C., *Transformed by the Light: Life after Near-Death Experiences*, Bantam, 1996.

7. Informed healing

23. Pert, C., ed. Ian Gawler, *Molecules of Emotion. Science and Passion of Healing*, The Gawler Foundation, 1997.
Pert, C., *Molecules of Emotion*, Scribner Press, 1997.

24. Pert, C. and Ruff, M., 'Neuropeptides and their receptors: A psychosomatic network', *The Journal of Immunology*, August 1985, Vol. 135, No. 2.

25. Campbell, S., and Murphy, P., 'Extraocular circadian phototransduction in humans', *Science*, Jan. 1998, 279(5349): 396–9.

26. Cardini, F. and Weixin, H., 'Moxibustion for correction of breech presentation — A randomised controlled trial', *JAMA*, 1998, 280: 1580–84.

27. Braud, W., Shafer, D., and Andrews, S., 'Electrodermal correlates of remote attention: Autonomic reactions to an unseen gaze', *Proceedings of presented papers: 33rd Annual Convention of the Parapsychological Association*, 1990, pp. 14–28. Updated at 35th annual convention, 1992, pp. 7–21.

28. Schlitz, M. and Braud, W., 'Distant intentionality and healing: Assessing the evidence', *Altern. Ther. Health Med.*, 1997, 3(6): 62–73.

29. Sheldrake, R., *Seven Experiments That Could Change The World*, Riverhead Books, 1995.

8. Chinese medicine

30. Eckman, P., *In the Footsteps of the Yellow Emperor*, Cypress Book Company, 1996, p. 86.

31. Eckman, P., *In the Footsteps of the Yellow Emperor*, Cypress Book Company, 1996, p. xviii.

32. Swithenby, S., 'SQUID helmet revolutionises real time imaging of the brain', *Physics World*, October 1993, pp. 26–7.

33. Markovitz, J., Matthews, K., et al., 'Psychological predictors of hypertension in the Framingham Study. Is there tension in hypertension?' *JAMA*, 1993, 270(20): 2439–43.

34. Milligan, S. and Clare, A., *Depression and How to Survive It*, Arrow, 1994.

35. Redfield Jamieson, K., *Touched with Fire*, Free Press, 1996.

36. Denollet, J., Sys, S., et al., 'Personality as independent predictor of long term mortality in patients with coronary heart disease', *The Lancet*, 1996, 347(8999): 417–21.

37. Julkunen, J., Salonen, R., et al., 'Hostility and the progression of carotid atherosclerosis', *Psychosomatic Medicine*, 1994, 56(6): 519–25.

38. Kaplan, G., Wilson, T., et al., 'Social functioning and overall mortality: prospective evidence from the Kuopio Ischaemic Heart Disease Risk Factor Study', *Epidemiology*, 1994, 5(5): 495–500.

39. Oxman, T., Freeman, D., and Manheimer, E., 'Lack of social participation or religious strength and comfort as risk factors for death after cardiac surgery in the elderly', *Psychosomatic Medicine*, 1995, 57(1): 5–15.

40. Ketterer, M., 'Secondary prevention of ischaemic heart disease. The case for aggressive behavioural monitoring and intervention', (*Review 58 refs.*) *Psychosomatics*, 1993, 34(6): 478–84.

41. Ornish, D., Brown, S., et al., 'Can lifestyle changes reverse coronary heart disease? The Lifestyle Heart Trial', *The Lancet*, 1990, 336(8715): 624–6.

42. Gould, K., Ornish, D., et al., 'Changes in myocardial perfusion abnormalities by positron emission tomography after

long-term, intense risk factor
modification', *JAMA*, 1995, 274(11):
894–901.

43. Linden, W., Stossel, C., and Maurice, J.,
'Psychosocial interventions for patients
with coronary artery disease: a meta-
analysis', *Archives of Internal Medicine*,
1996, 156(7): 745–52.

44. Ballegaard, S., Pedersen, F., et al., 'Effects
of acupuncture in moderate, stable
angina pectoris: a controlled study', *J.
Intern. Med.*, 1990, 227(1): 25–30.

45. Richter, A., Herlitz, J. and Hjalmarson,
A., 'Effect of acupuncture in patients
with angina pectoris', *Eur. Heart Journal*,
1991, 12(2): 175–8.

46. Cohen, S., Tyrell, D., and Smith, A.,
'Psychological stress and susceptibility
to the common cold', *NEJM*, 1991,
325(9): 606–12.

47. Kiecolt-Glaser, J., Malarkey, W., et al.,
'Negative behaviour during marital
conflict is associated with
immunological down-regulation',
Psychosomatic Medicine, 1993, 55(5):
395–409.

48. Harris, S. and Dawson-Hughes, B.,
'Seasonal mood changes in 250 normal
women', *Psychiatry Res.*, 1993, 49(1): 77–87.

49. Dawson-Hughes, B. and Harris, S.,
'Regional changes in body composition
by time of year in healthy post-
menopausal women', *Am. J. Clin. Nutr.*,
1992, 56(2): 307–13.

50. Well, M., *Civilisation and the Limpet*,
Perseus Books, 1998.

9. Healing patterns

51. Russek, L. and Schwartz, G., 'Narrative
descriptions of parental love and caring
predict health status in midlife: a 35-
year follow up of the Harvard Mastery
of Stress Survey', *Altern. Ther. Health
Med.*, 1996, 2(6): 55–62.

52. Pomeranz, B. and Stux, G., *Basics of
Acupuncture*, Springer, 1995.

53. 'National Institutes of Health
Consensus Development Statement',
Acupuncture, November 1997.

54. *Time*, 17 November 1997.

55. Cohen, M., Behrenbruch, C., and Cosic,
I., 'Shared frequency components
between Schumann Resonances, EEG
spectra and acupuncture meridian
transfer functions', *Acupuncture and
Electrotherapeutics Research*, 1998, Vol.
23, No. 1, pp. 92–3.

56. Becker, R., Reichmanis, M., et al.,
'Electrophysiological correlates of
acupuncture points and meridians',
Psychoenergetic Systems, 1976, Vol. 1,
105–112.

57. Cohen, M., Voumard, P., and Birch, S.,
'Low resistance pathways along
acupuncture meridians have dynamic
characteristics', *Biomedical Engineering*,
1995, Vol. 7, No. 2: pp. 137–142.

58. Schumann, W., 'Propagation of very
long electric waves and of lightning
discharge around the Earth', trans. from
German by Z. Angew, *Phys.* 1952, Vol. 4,
pp. 274–480.
Sentman, D. and Volland, H.,
'Schumann Resonances', *Handbook of
Atmospheric Dynamics*, 1995, Vol. 1, No.
11, pp. 267–95.

59. Orville, R. and Henderson, R., 'Global
distribution of midnight lightning',
Mon. Weather Rev., 1986, Vol. 114,
pp. 26–40.

60. Collinge, W., *Recovering from Chronic
Fatigue Syndrome: A Guide to Self-
Empowerment*, Perigree, 1993.

61. Drici, M., Raybaud, F., et al., 'Influence
of the behaviour pattern on the nocebo
response of healthy volunteers', *Br. J.
Pharmacology*, 1995, 39(2): 204–6.

62. Bendetti, F. and Amanzio, M., 'The
neurobiology of placebo analgesia:
from endogenous opioids to
cholecystokinin', *Prog. Neurobiol.*, 1997,
52(2): 109–25.

63. 'A Randomised trial of propranolol in
patients with acute myocardial
infarction. 1. Mortality results', *JAMA*,
1982, 247(12): 1707–14.

64. Ruberman, W., Weinblatt, E., Goldberg,
J., et al., 'Psychosocial influences on
mortality after myocardial infarction',
NEJM, 1984, 311(9): 552–9.
Comments: Colquhoun, D., 'Secondary
prevention of myocardial infarction',
New Ethicals Journal, May 1999, pp. 67–
74, Adis Press.

10. Modern theories

65. Carpi, A., 'The Natural Science Pages',
John Jay College, City University of
New York. Accessed through: http://
web.jjay.cuny.edu/~NSC/index.htm.

66. Tittel, W., Gisin, N., Brendel, J., et al.,
'Experimental demonstration of
quantum correlations over more than
10 km', *Phys. Rev.*, 1998, A57: 3229.

67. Linden, N. and Popescu, S., 'On multi-particle entanglement', *Fortschr. Phys.*, 1998, 46(4–5): 567–78.

68. Buchanan, M., 'Why God plays dice', *New Scientist*, 22 August 1998.

69. Buchanan, M., 'Beyond reality', *New Scientist*, 14 March 1998.

70. De Jonge, A., *The Life and Times of Grigori Rasputin*, Coward, McMann and Ceoqheqan, 1982.

71. Gerber, R., *Vibrational Medicine*, Bear and Co., 1983.

72. Dumitrescu, I., 'Life energy patterns visible via new technique', *Brain/mind Bulletin*, 1982, Vol. 7, No. 4.

73. Sheldrake, R., *The Presence of the Past: Morphic Resonance and the Habits of Nature*, Park Street Press, 1995.

74. Benveniste, J., 'From water memory to digital biology', *The Scientific and Medical Network Review*, April 1999, 69, pp. 11–14. Also via www.digibio.com.

75. Rolfes, A., 'The phenomenon of indicator muscle change – an exploration of its validity and meaning', 1997, ISBN No 06466 319752.

76. Hesiod's *Theogeny*.

77. Lovelock, J., *The Ages of Gaia*, Oxford, 1989.

78. Gordon, A., Merenstein, J., et al., 'The effects of therapeutic touch on patients with osteoarthritis of the knee', *J. Fam. Pract.*, 1998, 47(4): 271–7.

79. Turner, J., Clark, A., et al., 'The effect of therapeutic touch on pain and anxiety in burn patients', *J. Adv. Nurs.*, 1998, 28(1): 10–20.

80. Ireland, M., 'Therapeutic touch with HIV-infected children: a pilot study', *J. Assoc. Nurses AIDS Care*, 1998, 9(4): 68–77.

81. Wirth, D. and Cram, J., 'Multi-site electromyographic analysis of non-contact therapeutic touch', *Int. J. Psychosom.*, 1993, 40(1–4): 47–55.

82. Rosa, L., Rosa, E., Sarner, L., and Barrett, L., 'A close look at therapeutic touch', *JAMA*, 1998, 279: 1005–10.

83. Electronic responses to J. Tanne, 'Therapeutic touch fails test', *British Medical Jounal*, 98: 316: 1037. Sarner L., 20 Aug. 1999. Accessed through www.bmj.com/cgi/eletters/316/7137/1037/n.

84. Sagan, C., *The Demon-Haunted World: Science as a Candle in the Dark*, Random House, 1996.

85. Stevenson, I., *Where Reincarnation and Biology Intersect*, Praeger, 1997.

11. Healing in the twenty-first century

86. Lazarou, J., Pomeranz, B., et al., 'Incidence of adverse drug reactions in hospitalised patients: a meta-analysis of prospective studies, *JAMA*, 1998, 279(15): 1200–5. Also from WHO data.

87. WHO data. Todar, K., and Harms, J., 'Tuberculosis', University of Wisconsin. Accessed through www.bact.wise.edu/microtextbook/disease/tuberculosis.html.

88. Zuger, A., *New York Times*, 11 Jan. 1999.

Recommended reading

Ackerman, D., *A Natural History of the Senses*, Vintage Books, 1991.
Adams, P. (with M. Mylander), *Gesundheit!*, Healing Arts Press, 1993.
Bauby, J-D., *The Diving-Bell and the Butterfly*, Fourth Estate, 1997.
Becker, R. and Selden, G., *The Body Electric: Electromagnetism and the Foundation of Life*, William Morrow and Co., 1987.
Brown, C., *Optimum Healing*, Rider Books, Random House, 1998.
Buckman, R. and Sabbagh, K., *Magic or medicine? An investigation into Healing*, Macmillan, 1993.
Capra, F., *The Tao of Physics*, Flamingo, 1983.
Capra, F., *The Web of Life*, HarperCollins, 1996.
Cassell, E., *The Nature of Suffering*, New York, Oxford University Press, 1991.
Chopra, D., *Quantum Healing*, Bantam Books, 1990.
Dossey, L., *Healing Words: The Power of Prayer and the Practice of Medicine*, Harper San Francisco, 1995.
Dossey, L., *Reinventing Medicine*, Harper San Francisco, 1999.
Dossey, L., *Space, Time and Medicine*, Shambala Publications, 1982.
Eckman, P., *In the Footsteps of the Yellow Emperor*, Cypress Book Company, 1996.
Eisenberg, D. and Wright, T., *Encounters with Qi*, Penguin, 1985.
Gawler, I., *You Can Conquer Cancer: Prevention and Management*, Hill of Content, 1994.
Gerber, R., *Vibrational Medicine*, Bear and Co, 1988.
Kapchuk, T., *The Web that has no Weaver*, Rider, 1983.
Kubler-Ross, E., *On Death and Dying*, Macmillan, 1970.
Kubler-Ross, E., *The Wheel of Life*, Bantam Press, 1997.
Lovelock, J., *The Ages of Gaia*, Oxford, 1989.
Milligan, S. and Clare, A., *Depression and How to Survive It*, Arrow, 1994.
Morse, M. and Perry, P., *Transformed by the Light: The Powerful Effect of Near Death Experiences on People's Lives*, Mass Market Paperbacks, 1994.
Moyers, B., *Healing and the Mind*, HarperCollins, 1993.
Needleman, J., *The Way of the Physician*, Arkana, 1985.
Peck, M.S., *In Search of Stones*, Simon & Schuster, 1996.
Pert, C., *Molecules of Emotion*, Scribner Press, 1997.
Pomeranz, B. and Stux, G., *Basics of Acupuncture*, Springer, 1995.
Redfield Jamieson, K., *Touched with Fire*, Free Press, 1996.
Ring, K., *Lessons from the Light: What we can learn from Near Death Experiences*, Insight Books, 1998.
Rinpoche, S., *The Tibetan Book of Living and Dying*, Rider Books, 1994.
Sagan, C., *The Demon-Haunted World: Science as a Candle in the Dark*, Random House, 1996.
Sheldrake, R., *Seven Experiments That Could Change The World*, Riverhead Books, 1995.
Sheldrake, R., *The Presence of the Past: Morphic Resonance and the Habits of Nature*, Park Street Press, 1995.
Spiegel, D., *Living Beyond Limits*, Vermilion, 1994.
Stevenson, I., *Where Reincarnation and Biology Intersect*, Praeger, 1997.
Sutherland, C., *Transformed by the Light: Life after Near-Death Experiences*, Bantam, 1996.
Thich Nhat Hanh, *Living Buddha, Living Christ*, Rider, 1995.

PERSONAL NOTES

PERSONAL NOTES